Community Economic Development and Social Work

Community Economic Development and Social Work has been co-published simultaneously as *Journal of Community Practice*™, Volume 5, Numbers 1/2 1998.

The *Journal of Community Practice*™ Monographs/"Separates"

African American Community Practice Models, edited by Iris
Carlton-LaNey and N. Yolanda Burwell

Community Practice: Conceptual Models, edited by Marie Weil

Community Practice: Models in Action, edited by Marie Weil

Community Economic Development and Social Work, edited by
Margaret S. Sherraden and William A. Ninacs

These books were published simultaneously as special thematic issues of
the *Journal of Community Practice*™ and are available bound separately.
Visit Haworth's website at http://www.haworthpressinc.com to search our
online catalog for complete tables of contents and ordering information for
these and other publications. Or call 1-800-HAWORTH (outside US/Canada:
607-722-5857), Fax: 1-800-895-0582 (outside US/Canada: 607-771-0012),
or e-mail: getinfo@haworthpressinc.com

Community Economic Development and Social Work

Margaret S. Sherraden
William A. Ninacs
Editors

Community Economic Development and Social Work has been co-published simultaneously as *Journal of Community Practice*TM, Volume 5, Numbers 1/2 1998.

The Haworth Press, Inc.
New York • London

Community Economic Development and Social Work has been
co-published simultaneously as *Journal of Community Practice*™,
Volume 5, Numbers 1/2 1998.

The development, preparation, and publication of this work has been undertaken with great care.
However, the publisher, employees, editors, and agents of The Haworth Press and all imprints of
The Haworth Press, Inc., including The Haworth Medical Press and Pharmaceutical Products Press,
are not responsible for any errors contained herein or for consequences that may ensue from use of
materials or information contained in this work. Opinions expressed by the author(s) are not neces-
sarily those of The Haworth Press, Inc.

The Haworth Press, Inc., 10 Alice Street, Binghamton, NY 13904-1580 USA

Cover design by Thomas J. Mayshock Jr.

Library of Congress Cataloging-in-Publication Data

Community economic development and social work / Margaret S. Sherraden, William A. Ninacs,
editors.
     p. cm.
    "Has been co-published simultaneously as Journal of community practice, Volume 5,
Numbers 1/2 1998."
    Includes bibliographical references and index.
    ISBN 0-7890-0506-9 (alk. paper)
    1. Social service. 2. Community development–Economic aspects. 3. Economic development.
I. Sherraden, Margaret S. II. Ninacs, William A. III. Journal of community practice.
HV40.C622 1998
361.8–dc21   98-17895
                                                                 CIP

INDEXING & ABSTRACTING

Contributions to this publication are selectively indexed or abstracted in print, electronic, online, or CD-ROM version(s) of the reference tools and information services listed below. This list is current as of the copyright date of this publication. See the end of this section for additional notes.

- *Alternative Press Index,* Alternative Press Center, Inc., P.O. Box 33109, Baltimore, MD 21218-0401

- *Applied Social Sciences Index & Abstracts (ASSIA) (Online: ASSI via Data-Star) (CDRom: ASSIA Plus),* Bowker-Saur Limited, Maypole House, Maypole Road, East Grinstead, West Sussex RH19 1HH, England

- *caredata CD: the social and community care database,* National Institute for Social Work, 5 Tavistock Place, London WC1H 9SS, England

- *CINAHL (Cumulative Index to Nursing & Allied Health Literature, in print, also on CD-ROM from CD PLUS, EBSCO, and SilverPlatter, and online from CDP Online (formerly BRS), Data-Star, and PaperChase (Support materials include Subject Heading List, Database Search Guide, and instructional video),* CINAHL Information Systems, P.O. Box 871/1509 Wilson Terrace, Glendale, CA 91209-0871

- *CNPIEC Reference Guide: Chinese National Directory of Foreign Periodicals,* P.O. Box 88, Beijing, People's Republic of China

- *Economic Literature Index (Journal of Economic Literature) print version plus OnLine Abstracts (on Dialog) plus EconLit on CD-ROM (American Economic Association),* American Economic Association Publication, 4615 Fifth Avenue, Pittsburgh, PA 15213-3661

- *Family Studies Database (online and CD/ROM),* National Information Services Corporation, 306 East Baltimore Pike, 2nd Floor, Media, PA 19063

(continued)

- *Family Violence & Sexual Assault Bulletin,* Family Violence & Sexual Assault Institute, 1121 East South East Loop 323, Ste. 130, Tyler, TX 75701

- *Human Resources Abstracts (HRA),* Sage Publications, Inc., 2455 Teller Road, Newbury Park, CA 91320

- *IBZ International Bibliography of Periodical Literature,* Zeller Verlag GmbH & Co., P.O.B. 1949, d-49009 Osnabruck, Germany

- *Index to Periodical Articles Related to Law,* University of Texas, 727 East 26th Street, Austin, TX 78705

- *International Political Science Abstracts,* 27 Rue Saint-Guillaume, F-75337 Paris, Cedex 07, France

- *INTERNET ACCESS (& additional networks) Bulletin Board for Libraries ("BUBL") coverage of information resources on INTERNET, JANET, and other networks.*
  - <URL:http://bubl.ac.uk/>
  - The new locations will be found under <URL:http://bubl.ac.uk/link/>.
  - Any existing BUBL users who have problems finding information on the new service should contact the BUBL help line by sending e-mail to <bubl@bubl.ac.uk>.

  The Andersonian Library, Curran Building, 101 St. James Road, Glasgow G4 0NS, Scotland

- *National Library Database on Homelessness,* National Coalition for the Homeless, 1612 K Street, NW, #1004, Homelessness Information Exchange, Washington, DC 20006

- *National Periodical Library,* Guide to Social Science & Religion in Periodical Literature, P.O. Box 3278, Clearwater, FL 33767

- *Operations Research/Management Science,* Executive Sciences Institute, 1005 Mississippi Avenue, Davenport, IA 52803

- *Public Affairs Information Bulletin (PAIS),* Public Affairs Information Service, Inc., 521 West 43rd Street, New York, NY 10036-4396

(continued)

- ***Rural Development Abstracts (CAB Abstracts), c/o CAB International/CAB ACCESS . . . available in print, diskettes updated weekly, and on INTERNET. Providing full bibliographic listings, author affiliation, augmented keyword searching,*** CAB International, P.O. Box 100, Wallingford Oxon OX10 8DE, United Kingdom

- ***Sage Family Studies Abstracts (SFSA),*** Sage Publications, Inc., 2455 Teller Road, Newbury Park, CA 91320

- ***Social Work Abstracts,*** National Association of Social Workers, 750 First Street NW, 8th Floor, Washington, DC 20002

- ***Sociological Abstracts (SA),*** Sociological Abstracts, Inc., P.O. Box 22206, San Diego, CA 92192-0206

- ***Transportation Research Abstracts,*** National Research Council, 2101 Constitution Avenue NW, GR314, Washington, DC 20418

SPECIAL BIBLIOGRAPHIC NOTES

*related to special journal issues (separates)
and indexing/abstracting*

❑ indexing/abstracting services in this list will also cover material in any "separate" that is co-published simultaneously with Haworth's special thematic journal issue or DocuSerial. Indexing/abstracting usually covers material at the article/chapter level.

❑ monographic co-editions are intended for either non-subscribers or libraries which intend to purchase a second copy for their circulating collections.

❑ monographic co-editions are reported to all jobbers/wholesalers/approval plans. The source journal is listed as the "series" to assist the prevention of duplicate purchasing in the same manner utilized for books-in-series.

❑ to facilitate user/access services all indexing/abstracting services are encouraged to utilize the co-indexing entry note indicated at the bottom of the first page of each article/chapter/contribution.

❑ this is intended to assist a library user of any reference tool (whether print, electronic, online, or CD-ROM) to locate the monographic version if the library has purchased this version but not a subscription to the source journal.

❑ individual articles/chapters in any Haworth publication are also available through the Haworth Document Delivery Service (HDDS).

Community Economic Development and Social Work

CONTENTS

ABOUT THE EDITORS

Margaret S. Sherraden, PhD, is Associate Professor of Social Work and a Fellow at the Public Policy Research Centers at the University of Missouri at St. Louis. Her research and teaching focus on community development, immigration, health, and social policy. Her recent publications examine birth outcomes among Mexican immigrants in Chicago and social policy in Mexico. Currently, Dr. Sherraden is conducting qualitative research on low-income microentrepreneurs as part of a longitudinal study organized by the Self-Employment Learning Project of the Aspen Institute. She leads a community economic development task force for the Missouri Association of Social Welfare that is promoting community economic development in poverty areas of Missouri.

William A. Ninacs, MS CED, teaches Business Development in New Hampshire College's Community Economic Development (CED) Program, and he is a member of a worker cooperative through which he does research, training, and consulting. He is pursuing a PhD in social work at the Université Laval with a thesis on the types of empowerment found in CED initiatives. Mr. Ninacs is a former Chairperson of the Institut de formation en développement économique communautaire, a community economic development training organization in Montréal, and a founding board member of the Conseil québécois de développement social, a social planning and research council in Quebec. In 1985, he was hired to coordinate Quebec's first community development corporation. Prior to becoming a grassroots organizer, Mr. Ninacs had acquired over ten years' experience in accounting, auditing, taxation, financial management, human resource development, and strategic planning.

Introduction:
Community Economic Development
and Social Work

Margaret S. Sherraden, PhD
William A. Ninacs, MS CED

Urban and rural communities facing poverty, high unemployment, lack of infrastructure, environmental problems, and disinvestment often seem beyond help. Traditional welfare state policies provide assistance to impoverished and troubled families, but do little to help families and communities develop. In recent years, a variety of strategies that together are known as "community economic development" (CED) have responded to these problems by creating jobs, building locally-controlled asset bases, and strengthening the social fabric of communities.

We organized this collection to focus social work's attention on the exciting work of practitioners and scholars involved in CED, both nationally and internationally. Our objective is to increase knowledge about CED, to stimulate thinking about CED and its links to social work (and to community practice in particular), and to encourage research and curriculum development on CED in social work education. What is community economic development? Conceptualizations of CED vary a great deal. In large part this is because it is an emerging and dynamic field with many different currents (Bruyn & Meehan, 1987; Shragge, 1997; Douglas, 1994; Galaway & Hudson, 1994; Giloth, this volume). CED links social and economic development through the creation and regeneration of accessible institutions that empower and improve the life chances of community residents. Fundamental to CED is building and linking economic capital and social capital in communities. This involves creating economic oppor-

[Haworth co-indexing entry note]: "Introduction: Community Economic Development and Social Work." Sherraden, Margaret S., and William A. Ninacs. Co-published simultaneously in *Journal of Community Practice* (The Haworth Press, Inc.) Vol. 5, No. 1/2, 1998, pp. 1-9; and: *Community Economic Development and Social Work* (ed: Margaret S. Sherraden, and William A. Ninacs) The Haworth Press, Inc., 1998, pp. 1-9. Single or multiple copies of this article are available for a fee from The Haworth Document Delivery Service [1-800-342-9678, 9:00 a.m. - 5:00 p.m. (EST). E-mail address: getinfo@haworthpressinc.com].

tunity without separating it from social and civic concerns (Swack & Mason, 1987). In keeping with principles of good community practice, CED is indigenous; it is born in the community and residents take the lead in articulating goals, policies, and operations (Ninacs, 1993a; Weil, 1996). The focus of CED, particularly in social work, is on impoverished urban and rural areas (Peirce & Steinbach, 1987). Poverty, the distress following economic tremors, social and economic oppression related to gender and race, are but a few examples of the overriding issues that CED tries to tackle. To a great extent, CED's social component attempts to ensure that all members of a community can have access to the resources that they need to ensure their well-being.

Even though they share a common purpose, specific CED strategies vary enormously. For example, they may promote jobs and job training, homeownership, micro-enterprise or self-employment, business incubators, consumer and producer cooperatives, structures that encourage savings and investment, land trusts, commercial and industrial development, community infrastructure improvements, training and technical assistance, and supportive social services. CED activities bring together a wide constituency that includes community leaders, residents, community organizers, city planners, local business owners, bankers, and investors. Typically, activities are organized through non-profit, community-based development organizations that promote "economic empowerment and economic transformation for the poor" (Rubin, 1993, p. 431). Over the years, a number of umbrella organizations that provide networking, training, and advocacy for CED initiatives have also emerged.

CED aims to improve well-being at the individual, family, and community levels, both directly and indirectly. For example, individuals and families are often directly helped to open a small business or to obtain adequate housing. At the community level, more small businesses lead to more job opportunities as businesses expand (Bendick & Egan, 1991). Indirectly, increased homeownership may increase stability, pride, and social cohesion in the neighborhood. Other direct community-level effects are intangible. For example, community development corporations (CDCs) that build equity may not be as dependent on the whims of federal funding, leading to increased "capacity for community-directed change" (Rubin, 1993, p. 432). Some CED activities have also created opportunities for cooperative ownership, such as worker-owned businesses and collective housing. In the private sector, CDCs have been involved in promoting stock ownership in local enterprises. In these ways, non-profit and private enterprises become community-based, when ownership is widespread and local.

It is important to note that, although CED activities are "home-grown," few organizations and programs survive and thrive without subsidies. Indeed, research has shown that, although the economic side of CED ventures is self-sustaining, the social side most often is not (Ninacs, 1993b). Moreover, while financial support is essential in the early stages of development, the long-term nature of CED also requires programs that span the cycle from the initial mobilization to training, technical assistance, and research and development. Subsidies typically include funding and in-kind development support from federal, state, and local governments; private foundations; churches and religious groups; corporations, banks, and local businesses; and private donations (Peirce & Steinbach, 1987). Although an ongoing need for operating subsidies is often criticized, poor communities, having been the victims of disinvestment by both public and private institutions for many years, simply cannot come up with the considerable monetary resources needed for development (Halpern, 1993). However, poor families and poor communities can contribute to their development, through identifying and mobilizing other community resources (Kretzmann & McKnight, 1993).

The roots of CED lie in the social movements and community development efforts of the post-war period, as well as in innovative initiatives and experiences in other nations. In the United States in the 1960s, community-based organizations emerged in the context of the civil rights movement, local organizing, foundation initiatives, and increased federal legislation and funding for community development. Much of community organizing was devoted to gaining political power and channeling jobs and social services into poor communities. However, a first generation of CDCs also emerged at this time (Perry, 1987; Halpern, 1993). These organizations focused on commercial revitalization and housing projects in economically-distressed areas (Vidal, 1992). This marked the point when organizers began to see that access to capital and investment, in addition to jobs and income, were critical ingredients in community development. In the late 1970s, as federal funds became scarce and some questioned the benefits of large development projects, CED activists focused on smaller projects, such as rehabilitating rental and owner-occupied housing, promoting loans for small businesses, and retaining neighborhood jobs (Peirce and Steinbach, 1987).

Throughout this period, organizers in third world nations had been creating economic development programs, many of them on an even smaller scale. Confronted with considerably fewer financial resources, much of this development work is based on involving the poor in economic development. These international experiments include micro-credit and micro-enterprise, sustainable development, appropriate technology, self-help housing, land reform, in-kind contributions instead of payment for service, and savings strategies (Balkin, 1989; Otero & Rhyne, 1994; Yunus, 1987). These strategies are sometimes supplemented by provision of basic human services (nutrition, education, health, and housing). Developed nations have benefited in significant ways from these strategies. In fact, CED is one of the few areas of applied social sciences where diffusion regularly occurs from less developed to more developed countries (Midgley, 1995).

Social workers bring important skills to CED, including understanding how to facilitate groups, how to work at the grassroots level, how to work with residents in designing organizations and strategies that reflect local realities, how to work with federal and state authorities, how to locate resources, and how to deliver support services (Midgley, 1996). Social workers are also adept at identifying and promoting programs that incorporate features of indigenous institutions, such as rotating credit associations (Light & Rosenstein, 1995). But to be effective, social workers must become comfortable with the language and operations of CED. Understanding concepts and procedures of the world of business and finance is essential when organizing loan funds, supporting local business development, and encouraging urban revitalization. Skills such as basic accounting, budgeting, business and law, marketing, and strategic planning, to name a few, often need to be mastered. Familiarity with these is important because social workers will be asked to help clients and residents understand them. Social workers also must collaborate and be able to communicate with people who may work outside of our daily orbits, including bankers, business association leaders, real estate developers, labor union leaders, politicians, and urban planners.

This collection of research on CED opens with Bob Giloth's examination of the "rancorous" debate in the field of CED about whether we should be focusing on jobs, wealth, or place. In this lively article, he explores why controversy exists and how the debate might be conducted more constructively than it is now. Arguing that diversity of approaches is not a failure and that we need ways to understand what works, he begins to develop a theory of change. He introduces intriguing metaphors to describe the various dimensions of CED which should resonate and stir up creative responses among readers familiar with this field. The paper ends with a constructive proposal and research agenda for CED.

James Midgley and Michelle Livermore then explore the role of social work in promoting CED through creation and mobilization of social capital. They argue that social workers have the skills to mobilize social capital toward economic development through collaboration; organizational development; and mobilization of grassroots involvement, resources, and support. Indirectly, social workers can help create an environment that fosters external investment. However, they warn against several possible shortcomings, emphasizing that social workers must ensure that the interests and well-being of the poor are at the center of CED efforts, lest wealthier and more powerful constituents capture these new resources.

Three articles address micro-enterprise, a topic that has received a good deal of attention recently. Although pioneered abroad, micro-enterprise is a topic of increasing interest in the United States, especially as policy makers examine alternative job strategies for the poor in the policy shift away from guaranteed income support (Clark & Huston, 1993). Salome Raheim and Catherine Alter's study describes two U.S. micro-enterprise programs that assist public assistance recipients in self-employment. Their study analyzes the social and economic success of participants and finds that they are largely successful in objective terms, including increases in income and assets, job creation, and reduction of public assistance. In subjective terms, participants report improvements in well-being. Raheim and Alter make special note of the possibilities for increasing rates of business ownership among African Americans, which are generally low. Although this is a promising strategy overall, the authors caution that self-employment is a viable strategy for only a small percentage of the welfare population.

In an international example, Mahasweta Banerjee describes a micro-enterprise program initiated in a Calcutta slum in 1992. Placing the Indian program in an international context, she analyzes micro-enterprise success and impact through qualitative interviews with micro-entrepreneurs. She finds increases in income, employment, personal confidence, and an entrepreneurial culture, but writes that it may be too early to observe broader socioeconomic and political effects. Banerjee discusses the implications of her findings for micro-enterprise development, particularly with respect to welfare reform.

In another international example, Golie Jansen and James Pippard examine the Grameen Bank in Bangladesh, the earliest and best-known micro-enterprise program, founded by Mohammed Yunus in the mid-1970s. This article shows how one bank owned by poor women, run by poor women, and catering to poor women, can make a difference in everyone's lives on both economic and social fronts. They highlight the strategic importance of dealing with access to credit and micro-enterprise development in the struggle against poverty, and argue that self-employment options should be investigated by social workers interested in alleviating poverty here as well as abroad.

Turning to models that have been borrowed and adapted from developing nations, Evonne Lack and Dorothy Gamble assert that sustainable development should be brought into discussions of social and economic development. Using a snowball sample design, they identify and interview 59 leaders of sustainable development projects in the Southeastern United States, reporting on their activities, successes, challenges and training needs. Although they find that women predominate in these local development projects, respondents (including some men) report that women's effectiveness is limited because they are often barred from larger leadership roles and access to mainstream credit institutions and other resources. This article points to the need for legitimizing women's important roles in community development and improving access for these programs to financial and educational resources.

Jean-Marc Fontan and Eric Shragge explore the dilemmas facing CED intermediary organizations. Québec offers many interesting examples of CED practices in both urban and rural settings such as Community Futures Committees, youth service cooperatives, and training businesses. Unfortunately, they are not well known south of Canada's border. This article presents one urban model called corporations de développement économique communautaire (CDÉC). CDÉCs are similar to some U.S. community development corporations (CDCs) in that they are democratically-controlled, not-for-profit, local development organizations that oversee and support CED efforts by bringing together diverse groups to plan and coordinate development strategies in their communities. Through an analysis of services rendered by CDÉCs, Fontan and Shragge explore the contribution of CED intermediaries to social change and suggest that the adoption of different–and often contradictory–strategic perspectives seems inevitable in CED practice given the pressures exerted simultaneously by market, state, and community forces.

Housing is one of the key areas where CDCs have made a contribution. In a very balanced paper, Edward Scanlon first explores theoretical issues relevant to the use of home ownership as a strategy to fight poverty, and then ties in the findings of empirical research to illustrate how such an approach can be both advantageous and disadvantageous for low-income communities. He includes a presentation of fiscal, community development, and other policy implications of implementing low-income home ownership programs, and concludes that these could be complementary to CED strategies.

All of the articles in this collection point to the idea that CED is a planned, community-controlled process of social change by which disempowered communities, through new institutions, acquire control over the economic resources that they need to ensure individual and collective well-being. CED can thus be seen as a community empowerment process. The strategic importance of CED lies here, since empowerment is, at best, a shallow victory if economic, social, and political power is not fairly redistributed as a result of CED practice. Boothroyd and Davis (1993) believe that each CED initiative can be defined in terms of one of three approaches depending on whether "community," "economics," or "development" is its main dimension (indicated by an upper case letter): (1) cEd focuses on an economic growth paradigm and is primarily concerned with the production of goods and services; (2) ceD advocates structural change as a means of exerting control over market forces by reducing dependencies; (3) Ced follows a communalization mode to foster new expressions of solidarity and interconnectedness between individuals. However, no matter how CED is practiced, as these authors observe (p. 230), "the general objective is the same: to take some measure of control of the local economy back from the market and the state." But who gets the control and what do they do with it?

It can be argued that each of the three CED approaches produces a specific type of empowerment: economic growth favors self-empowerment, structural change opens the door to individual empowerment, and communalization encourages community empowerment (Ninacs, 1997). Self-empowerment is a conservative perspective that negates the need for a collective action since it sees individual self-interest as being the prime motivating factor driving relations between individuals, whereas individual empowerment (from a social work or a community psychology perspective) has to do with enabling individuals to overcome structural barriers and oppression, and thus requires structural change and collective action. The economic growth approach to CED favors self-empowerment since it seeks to remove barriers such as government regulations and bureaucratic constraints that impede entrepreneurial action. The structural change approach is focused on changing power relationships in society through democratic institution-building to provide victims of oppression and exclusion with access to resources and power. Indeed, the articles in this volume reveal promising answers to this question of control. We hope that social workers will examine CED practices to see how they can dovetail with other social interventions.

The articles in this collection illustrate the benefits of moving beyond anecdotal evidence to rigorous empirical research, and, as their authors suggest, considerable research is still needed. We have much to learn about fundamental theoretical and conceptual issues underlying CED initiatives, such as the respective role of the state and of the local community in ensuring social and economic well-being, the roles of social capital and of community capital in individual and collective empowerment processes, the social dimensions of savings and investment and of jobs and income, and the ways in which local economic initiatives can contribute to ensuring democracy and citizenship. We also have much to learn about designing more effective CED policies, paying attention to program impacts at policy and community levels. All types of data should be brought to bear on these questions, including quantitative and qualitative data that measure and interpret program effects. Further, special attention should be paid to the understudied impacts of race, ethnicity, and gender in CED (Betancur & Gills, 1993).

Much of CED's expertise is still in the field and not in the halls of academia, and this certainly weakens education about CED. We sincerely hope that academics, researchers, and practitioners will spend more time and energy examining CED's many facets, going beyond the buzzword definitions of community, empowerment, and development, so that we may all better understand how to acquire and use control over economic resources to make ours a more just world for all.

REFERENCES

Balkin, S. (1989). Self-employment for low-income people. New York: Praeger.

Bendick, M. Jr., and Egan, M.L. (1991). Business development in the inner city: Enterprise with community links. New York: New School of Social Research Community Development Research Center.

Betancur, J.J. and Gills, D.C. (1993). Race and class in local economic development. In R. D. Bingham and R. Mier (Eds.), *Theories of local economic development: Perspectives from across the disciplines* (pp. 191-212). Newbury Park, CA: Sage.

Boothroyd, P., and Davis, H. C. (1993). Community Economic Development: Three Approaches. *Journal of Planning Education and Research*, 12, 230-240.

Bruyn, S.T. & Meehan, J. (Eds.). (1987). Beyond the market and the state: New directions in community development. Philadelphia: Temple University Press.

Clark, P. & Huston, T. (1993). Assisting the smallest businesses: Assessing micro-enterprise development as a strategy for boosting poor communities. Washington, D.C.: Self Employment Learning Project, Aspen Institute.

Douglas, D. J. A. (1994). Community Economic Development in Canada (Volume One). Toronto & Montreal: McGraw-Hill Ryerson.

Galaway, B., & Hudson J. (1994). Community Economic Development: Perspectives on Research and Policy. Toronto: Thompson Educational.

Halpern, R. (1993). Neighborhood initiative to address poverty: Lessons from experience. *Journal of Sociology and Social Welfare* 20 (4), 111-135.

Kretzmann, J. P. & McKnight, J.L. (1993). Building communities from the inside out: A path toward finding and mobilizing a community's assets. Chicago, IL: ACTA.

Light, I. & Rosenstein, C. (1995). Race, ethnicity, and entrepreneurship in urban America. New York: Aldine de Gruyter.

Midgley, J. (1995). Social Development: The developmental perspective in social welfare. Thousand Oaks, CA: Sage.

Midgley, J. (1996). Involving social workers in economic development. *International Social Work* 39, 13-27.

Ninacs, W. A. (1993a). A synthesis of knowledge on community economic development. Briefing paper for Human Resource Development. Canada, Ottawa.

Ninacs, W. A. (1993b). Synthesizing the research results: Where is the common ground? *Making Waves* 4 (4), 18-20.

Ninacs, W A. (1997). The Bois-Francs Experience: Reflections on Two Decades of Community Development. In Community Economic Development: In Search of Empowerment and Alternatives (Revised Edition) (E. Shragge, Ed.). Montréal: Black Rose Books, pp. 147-181.

Otero, M. and Rhyne, E. (Eds.). (1994). The new world of microenterprise finance. West Hartford: Kumarian Press.

Peirce, N. R. and Steinbach, C.F. (1987). Corrective capitalism: The rise of America's community development corporations. New York, NY: The Ford Foundation.

Perry, S. E. (1987). Communities on the way: Rebuilding local economies in the United States and Canada. Albany, NY: State University of New York Press.

Rubin, H. J. (1993). Understanding the ethos of community-based development: Ethnographic description for public administrators. *Public Administration Review* 53 (5), 428-437.

Shragge, E. (1997). Community economic development: In search of empowerment and alternatives (revised edition). Montreal & New York: Black Rose Books.

Swack, M. and Mason, D. (1987). Community economic development as a strategy for social intervention. In Edward M. Bennett (Ed.), Social intervention: Theory and practice (pp. 327-347). Lewiston, New York, and Queenstown, Ontario: Edwin Mellen Press.

Vidal, A. C. (1992). Rebuilding communities: A national study of urban community development corporations. New York: Community Development Research Center, Graduate School of Management and Urban Professions, New School for Social Research.

Weil, M. (1996). Model development in community practice: An historical perspective. *Journal of Community Practice*, 3 (3/4), 5-67.

Yunus, M. (1987). Credit for self-employment: A fundamental human right. Dhaka: Grameen Bank.

Jobs, Wealth, or Place:
The Faces
of Community Economic Development

Robert P. Giloth, PhD

SUMMARY. Multiple and conflicting practices characterize the field of community economic development. Much of the debate about these practices revolves around different understandings of the importance of jobs, wealth, and place. No overarching definition, typology, or theory, however, offers a plausible way to resolve these conflicts about community economic development goals, levers of change, and practices. One promising approach engages the complexity rather than trying to simplify it. Metaphors are multivalent images that call attention to crosscutting issues, underlying assumptions, and hidden connections. Metaphors enable a richer and more creative reading of neighborhoods and economies when used in planning and design. This article explores six metaphors with relevance for community economic development: plugging the leaks, brokering connections, asset management, building ladders and webs, creating level playing fields, and enhancing markets. How to support this complex version of community economic development challenges the ways in which we encourage innovation, investment, and learning. *[Article copies available for a fee from The Haworth Document Delivery Service: 1-800-342-9678. E-mail address: getinfo@ haworthpressinc.com]*

Robert P. Giloth is Senior Associate at the Annie E. Casey Foundation. He has directed community development corporations in Chicago and Baltimore and is a regular book reviewer for *The Neighborhood Works*.

[Haworth co-indexing entry note]: "Jobs, Wealth, or Place: The Faces of Community Economic Development." Giloth, Robert P. Co-published simultaneously in *Journal of Community Practice* (The Haworth Press, Inc.) Vol. 5, No. 1/2, 1998, pp. 11-27; and: *Community Economic Development and Social Work* (ed: Margaret S. Sherraden, and William A. Ninacs) The Haworth Press, Inc., 1998, pp. 11-27. Single or multiple copies of this article are available for a fee from The Haworth Document Delivery Service [1-800-342-9678, 9:00 a.m. - 5:00 p.m. (EST). E-mail address: getinfo@haworthpressinc.com].

11

INTRODUCTION

At the 1986 annual meeting of the Center for Urban Economic Development (CUED) at the University of Illinois at Chicago, African-American activists carried on a spirited debate about the definition of community economic development. A retired steelworker who had fought against the closing of Wisconsin Steel on Chicago's southeast side argued for local and national steel authorities to reinvest in basic manufacturing in our cities, thereby creating and retaining livable wage jobs. A younger activist, from Chicago's devastated Englewood neighborhood, had a different perspective; he advocated entrepreneurship in inner-city communities of color.

This debate of 12 years ago illustrates one basic divide in the field of community economic development: jobs or wealth creation. Shortly before this meeting took place, the Chicago branch of the Local Initiatives Support Corporation (LISC)–a national community development and housing intermediary–had completed a study of neighborhood economic development in Chicago with help from the City of Chicago and a seasoned community developer as the researcher. LISC began with the assumption that neighborhood economic development was primarily about real estate or business development–place or wealth creation. A forum at the conclusion of the study, attended by a diverse group of 40 community developers, vigorously contested this narrow definition. Many argued that community economic development should include self help, employment training, and community organizing (Capraro, Ditton, and Giloth, 1985).

A 1990s manifestation of this debate pitted jobs against place-based development in Pittsburgh. The Tri-State Conference on Steel, formed in the early 1980s by church, community, and municipal leadership, established the Steel Valley Authority. This authority called for rebuilding the regional economy by using confrontational community organizing tactics, eminent domain, and a sectoral development approach. It has created or retained 2,000 jobs (Ferman, 1996). The Mon Valley Initiative emerged partially in response to Tri State, a project of LISC that would become a prime example of "consensus organizing" (Eichler, 1995). The Mon Initiative eschewed conflict and tried to develop a partnership among residents, organizations, and business elites, producing housing and commercial development. It has raised more than $16 million in investment and created 16 community development corporations, or CDCs (Mt. Auburn, 1996). Not surprisingly, both groups (the Steel Valley Authority and the Mon Valley Initiative) have roundly criticized the other as using bankrupt strategies that impede real community economic development.

These conflicts in definition, strategy, and constituency represent a small sample of the debate, and at times rancor, about community economic development. Reverse commuting strategies, for example, which connect people to suburban jobs, have been denounced as "urban apartheid" and as rewarding urban disinvestment and the relocation of firms to the suburbs (Lemonides, 1996). Sectoral employment practitioners have critiqued place-based efforts, such as those of CDCs, as a model of "neighborhood resource delivery" rather than wealth creation (Clark and Dawson, 1995). A chorus of criticisms aimed at CDCs focuses on their inability to stimulate economic development and alleviate poverty (Lemann, 1993; Porter, 1995; Foster-Bey, 1992). Microenterprise programs have been criticized for meager impacts.[1] The traditional antagonism between community organizing and development has been reignited in debates about "living wage" ordinances and "jobs gap" studies, which address job quality issues.[2] In a broader sense, some progressive analysts critique community economic development as another form of "localism," which has minimal ability to ameliorate the effects of the global economy (Fainstein and Fainstein, 1987).

Debate likewise exists about why community economic development is so contentious. One reason is that we do not have persuasive theories and related practices about how to ameliorate poverty–such as exist, for example, with the Grameen Bank and self employment in countries like Bangladesh, in which small amounts of credit to mostly women help overcome credit barriers and build family self-sufficiency and village economies (Counts, 1996). In contrast, poverty is increasing in the United States, old solutions seem to have failed, and evaluation studies show modest or no effects (U.S. Department of Labor, 1994).

A second reason is that different strategies have different constituencies: jobs relate to unions and progressive policy analysts; wealth creation attracts minority entrepreneurs, socially-responsible investors, and conservative policy-makers; and place attracts the community development movement as well as "bricks and mortar"-oriented municipal officials.

A third reason focuses on the modern, mixed economy in a period of governmental downsizing. In particular, for the past 20 years the United States economy has been lagging in growth and productivity, resulting in increased competition, innovation, and uncertainty. Because a "rising tide will lift all boats strategy" is not viable in the short run, there is a scramble for alternatives (Madrick, 1995).

In this article, I argue that the diversity of community economic development approaches does not represent a failure in definition or theory, but rather indicates a field of inquiry and action that requires different intellectual, planning, and investment tools. Consequently, I review salient variables that distinguish among different strategies, illustrate how multiple theories reflect the complexity of opportunity in the environment, discuss the use of "metaphors" in planning, and suggest some approaches for supporting multiple community economic development practices.

COMMUNITY ECONOMIC DEVELOPMENT– THEORY OF CHANGE

Resolving the debates about community economic development might occur through developing more inclusive definitions, typologies of practice, or perhaps even an overarching theory. Unfortunately, broad definitions of community economic development–such as targeting economic activity and benefits to particular populations in need–advance very little in resolving contested practices. Almost all approaches fit. Moreover, typologies of community economic development practices are either too simplistic or too complicated (they delineate many dimensions). In the later case, we have few examples of how these dimensions intersect. That is, we can create a map, but we have no direction. Finally, attempts at building a unifying theory of community economic development have floundered amidst the diversity of practices, unable to account for the variation of elements, relations, and impacts under different circumstances (Wiewel, Teitz, and Giloth, 1993).

Another approach recognizes community economic development's contextual nature and its many practice variations. Community actors develop theories of change concerned with economic well-being that are normative and action-oriented rather than explanatory. These theories guide good design in the future rather than explain what happened in the past. Such theories are frequently "organic" in that they derive from the experimentation of community actors as they interact in their local environments. Representing the choices, assumptions, and hypotheses of community actors, these theories identify problems, outcomes, pathways to change, and strategies (Rubin, 1993; Connell, Kubisch, Schorr, and Weiss, 1995).

What problems frame and motivate community economic development? Typical challenges range from a recognition of poverty (and its impacts such as crime, joblessness, and lack of access to resources) for particular classes of people such as women, community crises such as a plant closing or the deterioration of a commercial strip, or the appearance of dramatic opportunities–for example, nearby development that promises potential economic benefits.

Three outcomes distinguish the "ends" of community economic development: jobs, wealth, and place. These outcomes are interrelated and together provide a complete approach to the economic empowerment of the poor: jobs can be short-lived; wealth creation is long-term and focuses on business owners; and people come and go from places. Policy makers should decide which outcome(s) to focus on, based on the mission (values and vision) of community actors, analyses of the causes of the problematic situation, and the means (resources and technologies) available to fashion interventions.

A jobs focus increases access to the central means of livelihood in our society for particular classes of people, usually the unemployed or underemployed. Wealth creation enhances the business or asset-accumulating behavior of people or firms of a certain type—minority businesses, for example. Emphasizing place builds the locus of economic activity in specific geographic spaces not only to make economic benefits more accessible, but also to take advantage of community attributes such as location, social capital, culture, consumer base, and businesses and organizations. All three outcomes are plausible foci given the above problem definitions.

Likewise, there are three contrasting "pathways to change" that can produce jobs, wealth, or place outcomes: development, community organizing, and policy/planning. Each embodies a different "lever" for change, and consequently each makes different assumptions about the nature of social and economic transformation. Again, while not mutually exclusive, the political and organizational logic of these pathways produces quite different practice implications. Development pursues economic outcomes by engaging in business, real estate, human capital, or financial activities in the marketplace. Community organizing uses community power to affect economic outcomes related to the behaviors of institutions such as banks, developers, governments, and businesses. Policy and planning interventions change the legislative, institutional, and resource environments within which economic development takes place.

In reality, the three choices about problems, outcomes, and pathways are not sequential but are iterative as the design of community economic development unfolds. Strategies and projects emerge from a "messy" design process in which precipitating crises or opportunities and mission and values interact with a more nuanced analysis of barriers and opportunities, resources, and implementation requirements for success such as entrepreneurship. It is within this stage of "prototyping" innovations that the organic theory of change really takes form.

What makes theory-building of this sort even more difficult is the meaning of community. A common definition describes community as bounded geographic space defined by history, culture, administrative boundaries, convention, and social relations. But even poor communities that seem to fit this definition are not homogenous. For example, in the early twentieth century there was a vast difference between "slum" and "ghetto." The former was a starting place for poor ethnic immigrants; the latter was a constricted space largely for African-Americans (Philpott, 1978). In today's context, the severe social isolation of communities of "concentrated poverty" differ from "new immigrant" communities or from traditional working class communities that have suffered disinvestment (Massey and Denton, 1993).

Another definition of community focuses on groups of people regardless of geographic boundaries, such as women, youth, or the unemployed, who share common characteristics and face similar barriers. Strategies that serve these communities may be citywide or regional.

METAPHORS AND COMMUNITY ECONOMIC DEVELOPMENT PLANNING

A fundamental challenge is how to explore multi-dimensional phenomena–neighborhoods and economies–to develop organic theories of community economic development. Traditional analysis as well as contemporary strategic planning emphasize data gathering, goal setting, simulation, and decision-making, but are not very helpful in guiding synthesis of diverse information sources on behalf of designing interventions. In response, planners and organizational designers have explored the use of "metaphors" for building theories of change. Metaphors are multivalent images that call attention to salient and unexpected relationships, contrasts, analogies, underlying structures, levers of change, and opportunities (Schon, 1979; Senge, 1991).

Metaphors open windows on the critical parts of holistic phenomena. For example, municipal economic development can be understood as a *growth machine* or as *running a business*; organizations can be understood as *brains* or *machines* (Mier and Bingham, 1993; Morgan, 1987). Each metaphor conjures up different practices and implications. Some metaphors are called "generative" because they can be used to "generate" or invent possible modes of design or intervention (Schon, 1979). By reading or exploring a neighborhood or economy from the perspective of a number of metaphors, one finds a richer array of options and possibilities can be obtained to guide feasibility testing, project design, decisions, and learning by doing (Morgan, 1987).

Six metaphors provide a more comprehensive reading of the various dimensions of community economic development. Such a reading identifies a wide variety of theory of change elements and recognizes different community contexts. Moreover, these metaphors clarify the jobs, wealth, and place variations of community economic development. The six metaphors are: plugging the leaks; brokering connections; asset management; building ladders and webs; creating a level playing field; and enhancing markets. No doubt there are other metaphors that we could add to this list. I will consider each metaphor in some detail.

PLUGGING THE LEAKS

What if we thought of neighborhoods as having distinctive economies. In this scenario, local wealth–derived from exports and services–translates into circulating income spent on consumption, investment, savings, and the government sector. For example, one estimate for the Phillips neighborhood of Minneapolis suggests that this diverse neighborhood of 17,000 generates $800 million in economic activity each year (Meter, 1993). Unfortunately, this income "leaks" out of many neighborhoods by non-neighborhood spending, or is drained by absentee owners, some of whom can be quite exploitative (Gunn and Gunn, 1991; Hudson, 1996). Not surprisingly, the economies of poor neighborhoods have been compared to a "leaky bucket," "drained of resources," or even to an "internal colony."

The central problem or impact of "leaky bucket" neighborhoods is that circulating income does not produce multipliers; it doesn't bounce in the form of multiple neighborhood transactions (Center for Neighborhood Technology, 1986). For example, a family may buy at a local store that is, in turn, owned by a local resident who owns a home, saves at the corner bank, and also shops locally. In this case, income spent multiplies or bounces in the neighborhood. This multiplier of transactions does not happen as obviously when expenditures on goods and services are made outside the neighborhood or with absentee owners.

One way to think about community economic development, therefore, is as a "plugging the leaks" strategy, enabling local people and businesses to capture local income so that it bounces as many times as possible (Center for Neighborhood Technology, 1986; Morris and Hess, 1975). What this means for planning is that we must identify "leaks," test their feasibility for plugging, and then design and implement "plugging the leaks" strategies. Leaks of family income for consumer goods, housing, energy, taxes, or savings are quite common, although plugging strategies differ widely. Other leaks include non-local purchasing by businesses such as hospital complexes. A very common leak for poor communities is expenditure of local social welfare dollars devoted to residents of particular neighborhoods that are captured by non-local employees and businesses. A recent study of one low-income Chicago neighborhood, for instance, identified annual expenditures of $167 million for a population of 36,000 (Bush, 1996).

Plugging the leaks is an attractive community economic development strategy, but it has pitfalls. Neighborhoods do not really have separate economies; and they are inextricably linked to broader marketplaces. Providing competitive services may require economies of scale and service areas that eclipse neighborhood boundaries. Nevertheless, the "leaky bucket" is a potent image that helps explain why neighborhoods stay poor and how they might be transformed.

BROKERING CONNECTIONS

A common explanation for the persistence of poverty for individuals and neighborhoods emphasizes their social isolation from the mainstream (Massey and Denton, 1993; Wilson, 1987; Wilson, 1996). That isolation, or disconnection, means that people cannot take advantage of economic resources and opportunities.

Overcoming social and economic isolation requires brokering connections among poor communities and firms, regions, and resources. Two of these disconnections–spacial mismatch and informal networks–are particularly detrimental to increasing job access. Much recent metropolitan job growth has occurred in suburban locations because of technology, infrastructure, incentives, and racism. Yet, most of the jobless are from inner-city communities that have lower auto ownership rates and fewer viable public transportation alternatives. Indeed, many new suburban industrial enclaves are simply off the beaten path of public transportation (Hughes, 1993). Brokering geography may involve reverse commuting (Dewar and Scheie, 1995).

A second disconnection concerns the ways labor markets exclude inner-city job seekers. A great deal of hiring occurs through the "weak-tied networks" of existing employees rather than through formal labor market mechanisms such as advertising, placement agencies, and off-the-street walk ins. Firms reduce transaction costs by using their existing employees as "trusted" brokers who, in a sense, vouch for the reliability of their recommendations. This has become more prevalent as business owners lose contact and familiarity with urban neighborhoods; in some cases, firms even pay their employees to produce job referrals. For many inner-city job seekers, however, this process exacerbates the problem because they are disconnected as well from networks tied to existing employees (Mier and Giloth, 1985). Overcoming this barrier involves creating, becoming or knowing a trusted "employment broker" (Dewar and Scheie, 1995; Harrison, 1994; Melendez, 1996).

Brokering connections overcomes systemic barriers in the labor market that exclude, or diminish the returns to, poor communities. But the metaphor has broader implications as well—connections to key decision-makers, banks, funding streams, human service supports, the Internet, and for that matter, potential allies. In this sense, neighborhoods and their residents need to get "wired."

ASSET MANAGEMENT

Economic benefits derive from the strategic use of "valued resources" over time. Valued resources are assets. A paradigm shift in thinking about poor communities during the past few decades has recognized the limitations of focussing on the "deficits" of these communities and their residents—that is, what they lack. Instead many community developers are now committed to identifying, nurturing, and preserving the assets of poor communities (Kretzmann and McKnight, 1994).

Asset management emphasizes careful use of untapped neighborhood resources for community economic development. The metaphor suggests ways of thinking and acting about assets. First, communities have important economic assets that are often underused such as the entrepreneurial abilities and skills of residents, buildings, location, land, waste, organizations and associations, and financial resources. Residents, for example, have skills and experiences developed in family and associational life that can be translated into economic activity (Kretzmann and McKnight, 1994). Second, in more conventional economic terms, assets are those resources that have economic value and produce a financial return. Neighborhood assets include businesses and real estate. Third, assets require ongoing investment and attention to preserve and nurture their underlying value. Businesses, for example, require regular investment in people, technology, products, and markets if they are to remain competitive. Investment in assets, however, also suggests a rate of return. Finally, poverty researchers have concluded that the lack of asset (wealth) accumulation (homes, savings, etc.) among poor people accounts in part for the intergenerational transmission of poverty (Sherraden, 1991).

Asset management, in its various forms, suggests strategies and projects. Microenterprise builds upon local skills. Individual development accounts or "time dollar" schemes build the asset base of families. Life-long learning builds people capital over time. Land banking or "trusts" secures a scarce resource. Business succession programs protect existing organizational assets. Public "balance sheet" organizing focuses on the return to the community when public investments are made in assets. There are many other examples; the key is husbanding recognized and unrecognized community assets.

BUILDING LADDERS AND WEBS

Discrete solutions and individual interventions have proven inadequate for many social problems. Solutions require multiple components that unfold over time. And social interventions require the skills, resources, and experiences of multiple actors to be effective and sustainable. In other words, the design challenge is how to enable the growth of systemic changes.

Building ladders and webs metaphorically represents how to design such approaches, much like the work of carpenters and spiders. In the jobs arena, for example, there is increased attention to career ladders–transparent, step-by-step incremental increases in skills, responsibilities, and benefits in firms, sectors, and in the labor market generally. Such ladders have collapsed in recent decades. And given the new complexity of labor markets, the notion of career web may be more appropriate since people are likely to change jobs, firms, and sectors multiple times during their work lives (Dewar and Scheie, 1995; Giloth, 1995). The metaphor of ladders also applies to the incremental steps that may be needed for "harder to employ" groups to enter the labor market in the first place–family duties, volunteer work, part-time jobs, literacy and job training, and full-time work (Herr and Halpern, 1993).

Effective economic development also requires thinking about webs rather than single actors. We must pay attention to "clusters" of firms that share technologies, markets, and relationships. The question is how do members of clusters recognize that they are part of webs; and how do they act in concert around common interests related to workforce or marketing (Bosworth, 1996). As a consequence of downsizing, outsourcing, and globalization, the new form of corporate organization uses networks and webs, virtual organizations brought together in a flexible fashion to solve particular problems (Kanter, 1995). Similar webs and networks are found in successful, community-based employment and training programs that bring together employers, training and human service providers, and community residents (Harrison, 1994). Think of peer lending or savings groups as webs of relationships, in which peer association in small groups functions as the collateral for loans (Counts, 1996).

Building ladders and webs requires new ways of thinking and acting. Practitioners must see strengths in complementarity rather than competition and must feel comfortable with power-sharing rather than control.

CREATING LEVEL PLAYING FIELDS

Inner city residents, firms, and neighborhoods have not received fair access to resources and decision-making because of redlining, closed suburban housing, employment discrimination, or lack of public services. This limited access stems from intentional policies and incentives as well as from the unintended consequences of public and private actions.

Creating a level playing field enables communities to obtain equitable access to resources. Community organizing and policy advocacy around implementing the Community Reinvestment Act of 1977 (CRA) has perhaps been the premier effort to level the playing field for credit flows, mostly in the housing arena but increasingly for business lending (Immergluck and Bush, 1995). Attempts at creating "job linkage" mechanisms have ensured that community residents get fair access to jobs created by big development projects using public incentives (Mayer, 1989). Local government and institutional purchasing, particularly for small and minority firms, requires different forms of outreach, solicitation, and proposal evaluation criteria. That is, local companies may create more local economic benefits because of economic spin-offs even though their contract pricing may not be as competitive (SEEDCO, 1995).

A level playing field relates to "access" in all its dimensions: transportation, communication, inclusion, and power. One rationale for the creation of CDCs, for example, has been to create a level playing field of development capacity in poor communities so that they could pursue economic development opportunities (Perry, 1987). Conventional developers have left this playing field, in many cases, because of lower rates of return and greater uncertainty (Michelson, 1981).

Community organizing is fundamentally about creating a level playing field of politics by orchestrating community leadership, membership, and development of social capital (Cortes, 1993). Many communities have been left out of the halls of power, without the means to get their voices heard and be at the negotiating tables for important issues. Developing grassroots community leaders is a way to keep the playing field level.

ENHANCING MARKETS

Even poor neighborhoods are part of market economies in which goods and services are traded through a series of transactions. Many community developers display their myopia by not recognizing that markets exist in poor neighborhoods. The market is the problem, not part of the solution. For our purposes, then, market takes on a metaphoric dimension, calling attention to relationships and processes (mediated by financial and non-financial transactions) that occur in neighborhoods.

At the most simple level, residents and businesses buy goods, services, and assets (such as housing). From whom do they buy? And what are the benefits and costs of these transactions? An informal economy (both licit and illicit) also accounts for much neighborhood business and provides entrepreneurial training. Examples include back alley mechanics, tamale makers, or alley entrepreneurs who collect aluminum cans (Morales, Balkin, and Persky, 1995).

An even more unusual market is that of self-help and mutual assistance, what might be called the "social economy" of neighborhoods. These exchanges (which are mediated by cash, barter, and good will) deal with such services as child care, health, shopping, and home repairs. Some groups have tried to organize these transactions more formally into markets by establishing local currencies or "time dollars."[3]

Market activity rests on people engaging in "exchange" transactions, and in many cases, acting with entrepreneurial spirit. Community developers miss important opportunities when they ignore how markets currently work in neighborhoods or how they might be created or enhanced.

INFRASTRUCTURE TO SUPPORT MULTIPLE INNOVATIONS

There is no avoiding multiple versions of community economic development. Too many variables and choices characterize the field, and there are no obvious ways out of the complexity, through either better definitions, typologies, or an overarching theory. We have found, on the contrary, that organic theories of community economic development, anchored in the use of metaphors to understand communities and economies, enable people to think more creatively about the possibilities for increasing the economic development of jobs, wealth, and place. In other words, our way out of contentious battles among community economic development approaches requires greater, not less, understanding of neighborhood and economic diversity.

If this approach has merit, the question then becomes how we can better plan and manage the many variations and voices of community economic development. That is, can we identify the jobs, wealth, or place elements of various community economic development contexts. At the same time, it may be possible to diminish some of the rancor, unnecessary competition, and fashion-cycle funding.

Three potential remedies present themselves: informed pluralism, investor intermediaries, and field learning. Although each offers a distinct path, they are not mutually exclusive. The pluralist alternative is basically what exists now—many innovations that compete for limited resources. One might achieve marginal improvements in this free-for-all approach by developing better information about community economic development practices, better planning (through the use of metaphors), and continuing education for funders about investing in community economic development innovation.[4]

The intermediary alternative builds special-purpose social investors, of various shapes and scales, to invest in community economic development much as has been done for low-income housing. To a degree, LISC and the Enterprise Foundation, as well as community development banks and other local and national foundation initiatives, are developing such functions (Annie E. Casey Foundation, 1995). Intermediaries would more consciously invest with a concern for planning, training, evaluation, replication, and scaling up. They would be attentive to duplication, overlap and coordination, and innovation. The challenge, of course, is that community economic development, as we have defined it, is not a "cookie cutter" affair.

The learning alternative explicitly develops the community economic development field, with particular attention to the knowledge-development of practitioners as they pursue different strategies. A learning community acknowledges the experimental nature of its work, the opportunity for mutual learning, the need for an explicit learning framework, and the need for investment. The Aspen Institute has applied this approach to the microenterprise field and, now, for sectoral employment initiatives. An unanswered question is whether we can fruitfully initiate a learning approach across the subfields of community economic development—jobs, wealth, and place!

CONCLUSION

In 1998, foci on jobs, wealth, and place continue to represent contentious perspectives on community economic development. There are fewer good jobs, even as federal and state policy pushes for a version of welfare reform that places primary emphasis on work attachment without regard for job quality (Blank, 1995). Asset accumulation and wealth creation is highly uneven, particularly for African-Americans, thus reinforcing intergenerational poverty (Bates, 1993; Oliver and Shapiro, 1995). And there is growing consensus that the isolation and pathologies of concentrated poverty can only be overcome by building healthy communities.

Community economic development is multi-faceted and evolving, reflecting the complexity of neighborhoods and economies. Competition surely thrives because of different approaches, whether defined by a focus on jobs, wealth, or place. Our purpose should not be to reduce the complexity through oversimplifications or special interest advocacy, but to help community actors creatively engage the complexity and design better interventions for increasing economic empowerment.

NOTES

1. Small business researcher Tim Bates raised serious questions about the prospects of microenterprise approaches at a meeting on community economic development strategy convened in February 1994 by the Annie E. Casey Foundation.

2. Living wage ordinances have been sponsored in many cities and states. In Chicago the 1996 debates pitted community activists against community developers, particularly those who had a business constituency.

3. Edgar Cahn of the Time Dollar Institute in Washington, D.C. has developed an overall rationale and practice for the use of local currencies.

4. For example, the Neighborhood Funders Group, an affinity group of the Council on Foundations, is interested in creating a "toolbox" of promising community economic development practices related to workforce development and job creation. The group convened an educational conference on jobs for funders in February 1996.

REFERENCES

Annie E. Casey Foundation. (1995). *Annie E. Casey Jobs Initiative: Making connections.* Baltimore: Annie E. Casey Foundation.

Bates, T. (1993). *Banking on black enterprise.* Washington DC: Joint Center For Political and Economic Studies.

Blank, R. (1995). Outlook for the U.S. labor market and prospects for low-wage entry jobs. In D.S. Nightingale and R.H. Haveman (Eds.). *The work alternative:* Welfare reform and the realities of the job market (pp. 33-70). Washington, DC: The Urban Institute Press.

Bush, M., Ortiz, A. M., & Maxwell, A. (1996). *Tracking the dollars: State social service spending in one low-income community.* Chicago: The Woodstock Institute.

Bosworth, B.R. (1996). *Using regional economic analysis in urban jobs strategies.* Chapel Hill, NC: Regional Technology Strategies.

Capraro, J., Ditton A., & Giloth, R. (1985). *Neighborhood economic development: Working together for Chicago's future*. Chicago: City of Chicago.

Center for Neighborhood Technology. (1986). *Working neighborhoods: Taking charge of your local economy*. Chicago: Center for Neighborhood Technology.

Clark, P., & Dawson, S. (1995). *Jobs and the urban poor: Privately initiated sectoral strategies*. Washington DC: The Aspen Institute.

Cortes, E. (1993). Reweaving the fabric: The iron rule and the IAF strategy for power and politics. In H. Cisneros. (Ed.) *Interwoven destinies: Cities and nation* (pp. 294-320). New York: Norton.

Counts, A. (1996). *Give us credit*. New York: Random House.

Connell, J.P., Kubisch, A.C., Schorr, L.B., & Weiss, C.H. (1995). *New approaches to evaluating community initiatives: Concepts, methods, and contexts*. Washington, DC: Aspen Institute.

Dewar, T. & Scheie, D. (1995). *Promoting job opportunities*. Baltimore: Annie E. Casey Foundation.

Eichler, M. (1994). *Consensus organizing: Concept and background*. Boston: Consensus Organizing Institute.

Fainstein, N.I., & Fainstein, S.S. (1987). Economic restructuring and the politics of land use planning in New York City. *Journal of the American Planning Association, 2*, 237-248.

Ferman, B. (1996). *Challenging the growth machine: Neighborhood politics in Chicago and Pittsburgh*. Lawrence, KS: University Press of Kansas.

Foster-Bey, J. (1992). *Removing the barriers: An approach to increasing economic opportunity and reducing poverty*. Chicago: John D. And Catherine T. MacArthur Foundation.

Giloth, R. (1995). Social investment in jobs: Foundation perspectives on targeted economic development during the 1990s. *Economic Development Quarterly, 3*, 279-289.

Gunn, C., & Gunn, H.D. (1991). *Reclaiming capital: Democratic initiatives and community development*. Ithaca, New York: Cornell University Press.

Harrison, B. (1994). *Building bridges: Community development corporations and the world of employment training*. New York: The Ford Foundation.

Herr, T. & Halpern, R. (1993). *Bridging the worlds of Head Start and Welfare-to-Work*. Chicago: Project Match, Erikson Institute.

Hudson, M. (1996). *Merchants of misery*. Monroe, Maine: Common Courage Press.

Hughes, M.A. (1993). *Over the horizon: Jobs in the suburbs of major metropolitan areas*. Philadelphia: Public/Private Ventures.

Immergluck, D. & Bush, M. (1995). *Small business lending for economic development: Vol. 1: Strategic responses for urban communities*. Chicago. The Woodstock Institute.

Kanter, R.M. (1995). *World class*. New York: Simon and Schuster.

Kretzmann, J. & McKnight, J. (1994). *Building communities from the inside out*. Evanston, IL: Center for Urban Affairs, Northwestern University.

Lemann, N. (1994). The myth of community development. *New York Times Magazine* (June 9): 26-31;50;54;50.

Lemonides, J. (1996). "Urban jobs needed." Letter to the Editor. *The Neighborhood Works,* 1, 6.

Madrick, J. (1995). *The end of affluence.* New York: Random House.

Massey, D.S. & Denton, N.A. (1993). *American apartheid.* Cambridge, MA: Harvard University Press.

Mayer, N. (1989). Berkeley's city hall is "first source" when employers need workers. *Western City* (October), 40-44.

Melendez, E. (1996). *Working for jobs: The center for employment training.* Boston: Mauricio Gaston Institute.

Meter, K. (1993). *Phillips neighborhood: Income statement and balance sheet.* Minneapolis: Crossroads Resource Center.

Michelson, S. (1981). Community-based development in urban areas. In R. Friedman & W. Schweke (Eds.). *Expanding the opportunity to produce: Revitalizing the economy* through new enterprise development (pp. 534-549). Washington DC: Corporation for Enterprise Development.

Mier, R. & Bingham, R.D. (1993). Metaphors of economic development. In (Eds.), R.D. Bingham and R. Mier. *Economic development in the United States: Toward a Theoretical perspective* (pp. 284-304). Newbury Park, CA: Sage Publications.

Mier, R. & Giloth, R. (1985). Hispanic employment opportunities: A case of internal labor markets and weak-tied social networks. *Social Science Quarterly, 2,* 296-309.

Morales, A., Balkin, S., & Persky, J. (1995). The value of benefits of a public street market: The case of Maxwell Street. *Economic Development Quarterly, 4,* 304-320.

Morgan, G. (1985). *Images of organizations.* Newbury Park, CA: Sage Publications.

Morris, D. & Hess, K. (1975). *Neighborhood power.* Boston: Beacon Press.

Mt. Auburn Associates. (1996). *Study of model development intermediaries for the Annie E. Casey Foundation's jobs initiative.* Somerville, MA: Mt. Auburn Associates.

Oliver, M.L., Shapiro, T.M. (1995). *Black wealth/white wealth: A new perspective on racial inequality.* New York: Russell Sage.

Perry, S. E. (1987). *Communities on the way: Rebuilding local economies in the United States and Canada.* Albany, NY: The State University of New York Press.

Philpot, T. (1978). *The slum and the ghetto.* New York: Oxford University Press.

Porter, M. (1994). *Competitive advantage of the inner city.* Cambridge, MA: Harvard Business School.

Rubin, H. (1994). There aren't going to be any bakeries here if there is no money to afford jellyrolls: The organic theory of community development. *Social Science Quarterly 3,* 401-24.

Schon, D. (1983). *Reflective practitioner.* New York: Basic Books.

Schon, D. (1979). Generative metaphors: A perspective on problem-setting. In (Ed.), A. Ortony. *Metaphor and thought* (pp. 254-283). Cambridge, UK: Cambridge University Press.

SEEDCO. (1995). *Jobs and economic development: Capitalizing on opportunities in the health care sector.* New York: SEEDCO.

Senge, P. (1990). *The fifth discipline.* New York: Doubleday Press.

Sherraden, M. (1991). *Assets and the poor: A new American welfare policy.* Armonk, NY: M.E. Sharpe, Inc.

U.S. Department of Labor. (1994). *The role of job training in expanding employment opportunities and increasing the earnings of the disadvantaged.* Washington, DC: U.S. Department of Labor.

Wiewel, W., Teitz. M, & Giloth, R. (1993). The economic development of neighborhoods and localities. In R.D. Bingham and R. Mier (Eds.), *Theories of local economic development: Perspectives from across the disciplines* (pp. 80-99). Newbury Park. CA: Sage Publications.

Wilson, W.J. (1987). *Truly disadvantaged.* Chicago: University of Chicago Press.

Wilson, W.J. (1996). *When work disappears.* New York: Alfred A. Knopf.

Social Capital
and Local Economic Development:
Implications
for Community Social Work Practice

James Midgley, PhD
Michelle Livermore, PhD

SUMMARY. Although the concept of social capital has direct relevance to community practice, it is not widely known in social work. This paper defines the concept, traces the development of social capital theory, and examines ways in which community social workers can promote local economic development by enhancing social capital. It contends that community social workers can make a major contribution to local economic development by implementing projects that mobilize social capital and promote the material well-being of local people. *[Article copies available for a fee from The Haworth Document Delivery Service: 1-800-342-9678. E-mail address: getinfo@haworthpressinc. com]*

The concept of social capital is widely used to connote the importance of local community networks and associations in society. Popularized

James Midgley is Specht Professor and Dean, School of Social Welfare, University of California at Berkeley.

Michelle Livermore is Research Associate, Office of Research and Economic Development, Louisiana State University.

[Haworth co-indexing entry note]: "Social Capital and Local Economic Development: Implications for Community Social Work Practice." Midgley, James, and Michelle Livermore. Co-published simultaneously in *Journal of Community Practice* (The Haworth Press, Inc.) Vol. 5, No. 1/2, 1998, pp. 29-40; and: *Community Economic Development and Social Work* (ed: Margaret S. Sherraden, and William A. Ninacs) The Haworth Press, Inc., 1998, pp. 29-40. Single or multiple copies of this article are available for a fee from The Haworth Document Delivery Service [1-800-342-9678, 9:00 a.m. - 5:00 p.m. (EST). E-mail address: getinfo@haworthpressinc.com].

29

through the writings of Robert Putnum (1993, 1995, 1996), social capital gives expression to communitarian beliefs and extols the virtues of civil society. Putnum's research into civic involvement and political behavior in Italy (1993), and his more recent claim that America's civic traditions are being undermined by excessive exposure to television (1996) have brought the concept to the attention of politicians, journalists, civic leaders, business people, and informed members of the public. His ideas have also attracted attention from social scientists and professionals concerned with economic development.

Putnum's (1993) research in Italy, undertaken with two colleagues, reveals that regions with a high degree of civic engagement recorded significantly higher rates of economic growth than those with poorly developed civic traditions. Although this finding has primarily been used to explain variations in economic performance among different localities, it also informs the normative proposition that programs designed to promote social capital formation can enhance local economic development. This proposition implies that community organizers should not only seek to enhance associational activities for desirable social and political ends but should also seek to promote economic development.

Although community social workers have not been extensively involved in economic development, there is a growing realization that they need to engage in these activities (Midgley, 1996). The problems of poverty and deprivation require interventions that improve incomes and standards of living. Social workers are instructed by the National Association of Social Worker (NASW) *Code of Ethics* to "ensure that all persons have access to the resources, services and opportunities which they require" and to "act to expand choice and opportunity for all persons, with special regard for disadvantaged or oppressed groups and persons"(1995, p. 2629).

Social workers can apply their conventional knowledge and skills as community organizers to promote local economic development by using community organization techniques to foster social capital formation. This paper discusses ways in which community social work can generate social capital specifically to promote local economic development. It urges community organizers to transcend their conventional roles and promote activities that foster economic growth.

THE THEORY OF SOCIAL CAPITAL

Although Putnum popularized the term social capital, Coleman (1988) introduced it into the vocabulary of the social sciences as a part of his efforts to synthesize the individualist and sociological traditions. In his work, Coleman claims that these two traditions can be harmonized by focusing on the relationships formed among human beings. This synthesis accommodates both individual action and societal influences and permits social scientists to understand the complex ways people function within the context of wider societal institutions, norms, and values.

To Coleman, the term social capital connotes the social relationships, ties, and networks established among people within the context of wider social systems. He suggests that strong and enduring human relationships facilitate effective human functioning and improve the quality of societal institutions. He notes that social systems with a high degree of social capital have well-developed social networks and institutions and function more effectively than those with limited social capital.

Coleman also argues that there is a direct relationship between the volume of social capital and economic development. Like physical capital, social capital is productive. In other words, economic development is more likely to occur in social systems with strong social networks, well developed associations, and a high degree of civic engagement. Coleman argues that economic development is most likely to occur in social systems characterized by a high degree of civic trust. He also pays particular attention to the link between social and human capital. Economists such as Psacharopoulos (1973, 1992) have long argued that education is an investment in human capital and that high levels of educational attainment contribute to economic development. Developing this theme, Coleman contends that human capital formation is more likely to occur in social systems with a high degree of social capital. Reviewing empirical data, he shows that children from well-integrated families have higher educational achievements than those where relationships are weak or defective. Similarly, sectarian schools that encourage associational activities have higher educational attainments than public schools that do not emphasize these activities. In these situations, a high degree of social capital is conducive to high educational attainment, human capital formation, and higher economic performance.

Coleman's work draws on a well-established body of sociological writing that emphasizes the importance of relationships, associational activities, and institutions for societal well-being. These ideas have been applied at different levels of sociological analysis including studies of the quality of relationships among individuals, community level analyses and large-scale investigations into the effectiveness of associations at the societal level. Examples of research that have focused on these issues include Granovetter's (1974) study of how people use social ties to find employment; Wilson's (1987) account of 'underclass' communities where isolation and poorly developed association activities correlate with a high incidence of poverty and crime; and Putnum's (1993) research, mentioned earlier, which found that regions of Italy with high levels of civic engagement have significantly higher rates of economic growth than those where associational involvement is low.

Like Coleman's own work, these studies reflect older ideas in the social sciences. Tocqueville's analysis of American political and civic activities in the 1830s is a formative influence as is the work of Durkheim, whose concern with social harmony and integration informs the belief that extensive social interaction enhances social well-being. The studies of social disorganization by the Chicago School of Urban Sociology in the 1920s provide a basis for current accounts of the negative consequences of a lack of social capital in deprived communities.

The notion of social capital is also consonant with well-established communitarian and populist themes in American culture. Although the term social capital is not widely used in communitarian literature, it reflects the communitarian belief that extensive associational engagement at the local level brings positive social benefits (Etzioni, 1993). While Putnam's early writing did not explicitly reference communitarianism, a communitarian influence has become more evident in his later work that laments the decline of community in America (Putnum, 1995, 1996).

It should be noted that there are other definitions of social capital. Midgley (1995) defines social capital as social infrastructure, suggesting that infrastructural development for social purposes not only provides the material amenities needed for community development but also creates the community-held assets that bring people together and enhance their commitment to local development. Sherraden (1991) presents a similar idea. Although he focuses primarily on individually held assets such as Individual Development Accounts, he recognizes the importance of community assets, such as revolving community loan funds, in generating economic development at the local level.

While social capital theory has important implications for local economic development, it does not clearly specify which associational activities translate into economic development. The ideas contained in the literature on social capital still need to be systematically developed into a comprehensive explanatory model. For example, Coleman's view that the social trust generated by enhanced social capital promotes economic activity also needs to be elaborated. Fukuyama's recent (1995) work is a step in this direction.

Fukuyama argues that the large-scale economic organizations can only function effectively if their individual members establish relationships based on a shared commitment to moderating self-interest and to collaborating to foster economic progress. Banks, factories, commercial firms, and similar organizations cannot gain the confidence of their clients and staff if they are perceived as ruthless, exploitative, and exclusively committed to maximizing profits. While the profit motive does indeed motivate people, it must be moderated by trust. In the absence of trust, commercial operations invariably fail and harm economic progress. Economic life is not simply a matter of pursuing profits and economic interests but of maximizing what Fukuyama calls 'spontaneous sociability' in economic relations. Countries that promote trust in economic relations are most likely to prosper. Those that encourage a 'greed is good' philosophy will fail and decline.

In addition to more detailed elaboration, the application of social capital ideas to local economic and social development requires greater normative refinement. The proposition that extensive civic engagement results in greater economic growth needs to be accompanied by policy recommendations for promoting particular associational activities conducive to development. Analytical speculation can only result in positive policy application by showing how community social workers can enhance social capital to promote local economic development. This paper seeks to make a modest contribution to this endeavor.

SOCIAL CAPITAL, COMMUNITY SOCIAL WORK AND LOCAL ECONOMIC DEVELOPMENT

As noted earlier, local economic development has not been the primary focus of community social workers. Instead, they have been largely concerned with enhancing people's participation, coordinating and building coalitions among local organizations, and organizing people to campaign for improved services. While these empowerment activities are appropriate forms of community practice, there is increasing recognition that the profession must also engage in activities that address the need for economic development at the local level (Midgley and Simbi, 1993; Midgley, 1996). This paper argues that social workers can use their existing skills and knowledge to promote local economic development by mobilizing social capital.

Building Social Capital Through Community Organization

Social workers are already involved in creating social capital through conventional community organization techniques. These techniques typically involve defining the target community or population, identifying and analyzing community resources and problems, creating local community agencies, facilitating setting goals and objectives, selecting effective strategies for community action, implementing programs and projects, and evaluating outcomes (Cox, 1995; Netting, Kettner, and McMurtry, 1993; Rothman, 1995; Rubin and Rubin, 1992). Community organizers work with local leaders, civic groups, local businesses, libraries, neighborhood watch groups, churches, women's groups, homeowner's associations, schools, and youth organizations to form and strengthen associations, increase civic engagement, strengthen social networks, help residents develop a sense of identity, encourage effective collaboration, recruit new membership, and handle pressing social problems.

As community social workers work with these groups, they bring divergent community members together around common interests and thus enhance networks and social capital formation. By building coalitions among people and organizations with divergent interests, community social workers create new social relationships and associations and strengthen people's participation in community affairs. Social workers play a particularly important role in social capital formation by recruiting participants from all segments of the community. By building relationships among individuals from different social classes and ethnicities, they increase the density of social networks. They also encourage otherwise disenfranchised individuals to become involved in civic life by creating associations that value divergent views and address concerns that affect diverse constituencies.

The result of these activities is the creation and strengthening of associations, the promotion of civic engagement, the enhancement of personal networks, and a net increase in social capital. By creating social capital, community social workers are poised to direct social capital towards economic development.

Directing Social Capital Towards Economic Development

As Blakely (1994) shows, those concerned with local economic development use various strategies to promote economic revitalization of communities. They seek to regenerate local businesses or encourage new businesses to relocate into the community. In either case, they are concerned with marketing and identifying potential consumers. They target local consumers or seek to draw consumers to the community to purchase goods and services. They also export locally produced goods and services to consumers outside the community. These strategies are designed to generate economic production within the community, to create local employment, and to increase local standards of living.

The success of these strategies depends on both economic and social factors. A manufacturing facility that relocates into a poor community must be able to hire workers who have the skills and commitment to ensure its viability. Similarly, the revitalization of local enterprises requires that local people support these enterprises. There is little point in opening a local grocery store if people choose to shop at supermarkets located outside the community. Similarly, communities with high crime rates and marked social deterioration are unlikely to attract external investment.

Social factors such as these are relevant to the promotion of local economic development. Economic strategies alone are unlikely to succeed in communities marked by high rates of unemployment and crime, blighted schools and homes, and the emigration of educated people to the suburbs. These communities critically need social interventions designed to support local economic development. By enhancing social capital formation in these communities, social workers can help in ensure that economic strategies succeed.

Creation of social capital, however, is only a first step in promoting local economic development. Social workers must not only be able to enhance social capital but must also direct social capital specifically towards economic activities. The networks, associations, and civic activities they enhance must be directed toward this goal. This is best accomplished when social workers collaborate with urban planners, political leaders, and local community members concerned with local economic development. The community development corporation is a key vehicle for promoting effective developmental engagement. These organizations are comprised of local people, representatives of local associations, and other concerned parties; they are an important element in social capital formation for local economic development. If such an organization does not already exist, social workers can make an important contribution by helping to establish one. If an organization of this kind does exist, social workers can become actively involved in supporting and strengthening its activities.

While urban planners are well qualified to identify strategies for promoting local economic development, social workers can mobilize support for these activities and use their networks with local associations, churches, and other groups to create a wider awareness of the need for local economic projects. They can facilitate community meetings and discussions at church, youth, women's and other local groups. In this way, social workers can foster an awareness of the need for development and begin to suggest ways in which local people can actively engage in economic renewal.

In addition to increasing support for and participation in local economic development, social workers can use social capital to stimulate greater local involvement in small business development. By working with other professionals, social workers can help to create new enterprises and strengthen existing businesses (Livermore, 1996). Third World social workers already have extensive experience in this field and their activities are now emulated by social workers in the industrial nations (Balkin, 1989; Else and Raheim, 1992). They can play a particularly important role in encouraging low-income women to start micro-enterprises (Dignard and Havet, 1995). Also, their knowledge and skills with groups give them special skills in fostering cooperative ventures. The use of peer lending, for instance, has proven an effective mechanism for involving people in these enterprises.

Social workers have a similar role to play in strengthening existing businesses in the community. Despite the frequency of economic stagnation in the poorest communities, existing small businesses can be sustained and expanded. However, local enterprises need the support of the community. When local consumers use supermarkets and other large retail outlets outside the community, local businesses decline. To counter this trend, social workers can assist local businesses to form a local business association that can collaborate with the community economic development agency to formulate strategies for business revitalization. This form of social capital creation has a direct impact on economic development. Social workers can also assist in developing and implementing a community marketing strategy that encourages local people to support local businesses. This strategy involves community awareness and participation campaigns as well as meetings with local associations, churches, and other forums.

Social workers can also use their skills to attract greater external investment. Their abilities to network and lobby should be used to persuade firms to relocate or invest in the community and to persuade political leaders and financial institutions to support local economic activities. Social workers should be actively involved in securing resources for local economic development in terms of the Community Reinvestment Act of 1977. This act requires banks and trusts to loan money to qualified applicants and end the practice of redlining, whereby discrimination prevents investment in certain geographic areas (Thomas, 1994).

Social workers have an important contribution to make in using social capital for job training and placement. Although the need for job training has long been recognized, a great deal still needs to be done to create effective opportunities for local people from deprived communities to upgrade their skills. Many are reluctant to admit that they are poorly educated and many are intimidated by formal educational institutions. Social workers can encourage local associations to create educational programs suited to the needs of local people. Local associations may provide more effective job training than is currently provided by formal educational institutions.

Social workers can also foster links between employers and job seekers through social networks and associations. They can encourage local groups to engage more effectively in job referral activities. Granovetter's (1974) research has shown that most people use personal network ties to find employment. Although they peruse advertisements as well, networks are the most effective means of finding a job. By creating employment referral networks through local churches, civic associations, and youth and women's groups, social workers can effectively use social capital to link people with jobs.

As noted earlier, social capital involves more than the creation of personal networks and civic associations. Midgley (1995) and Sherraden (1991) discuss ways in which social workers can direct social capital towards economic development goals. As Midgley notes, social workers in Third World countries have extensive experience in developing social infrastructure in local communities. He and Simbi (1993) argue that community social workers in the United States have much to learn from the experiences of these colleagues. Similarly, Sherraden's proposals for asset accumulation have direct relevance to social work involvement in local economic development. The creation of individual development accounts (IDAs) at the local level and the promotion of community assets also foster local economic development.

Social capital can also make an indirect contribution to local economic development. For example, the ameliorative impact of social capital formation on local community problems such as substance abuse and crime will improve local business development. In many communities, small business growth is retarded by high levels of crime and other social problems. Economic development is more likely to succeed in areas where these problems are controlled. The existence of well-developed associations, clubs, and other amenities is also likely to attract external investment and residents into communities experiencing revitalization. Increased social capital also enhances meaningful social relations and trust among people. As noted earlier, the creation of trust is a vital component of social capital formation that has a powerful although indirect impact on community economic development (Fukuyama, 1995).

LIMITATIONS OF THE SOCIAL CAPITAL APPROACH

As this paper has shown, social capital theory provides a useful framework for social work's efforts to contribute to local economic development. This involves the re-direction of conventional community organization techniques to create social capital specifically to enhance local economic development. However, social capital theory has limitations that social workers need to recognize. These limitations are not only found in the technical challenges of implementing social capital ideas, but also in wider social, political, and economic issues. These issues affect social work's commitment to eradicate poverty and promote social justice.

For example, there is a danger that local economic development will fail to include the majority of the population in the development process. As is well known, economic development does not automatically 'trickle down' to the poor (Fields, 1980). For this reason, community social workers must ensure that economic activities do not focus only on the best educated and most organized groups. In addition, social workers must guard against local leaders expropriating development activities for themselves. As Fisher (1994) points out, many Community Development Corporations in the 1970s were more concerned with creating profits than with alleviating poverty. As a result, they promoted minority middle class interests rather than revitalizing poor neighborhoods.

Local efforts to create social capital and promote development may endorse the belief that solutions to community decline can only be found locally. This idea can leave poor communities with no external resources to deal with their problems. For instance, retrenchments in government assistance for community development over the past 15 years have created enormous problems for low-income neighborhoods. The idea that creating social capital at the local level can solve local problems may legitimize further inaction. In the light of current anti-tax sentiments and the prevalence of racist attitudes towards inner-city poor, indifference to impoverished communities is widespread. Social workers need to redouble their efforts to campaign for investments to revitalize these communities.

A related problem is that the concept of social capital can be expropriated by the political right for ideological ends. In a vigorous critique of Putnum's work, Skocpol (1996) shows how right-wing groups have cynically exploited communitarian ideas to gain electoral advantage. As the crass individualism that characterized the Reagan era loses popular appeal, these groups increasingly use communitarianism to package right wing ideology. Right-wing think tanks and magazines now make frequent reference to social capital theory to claim that the revitalization of America's civic traditions offers an alternative to the 'failed' statism of the New Deal. They also use these ideas to argue that government intervention is not needed to find solutions to the country's social ills. It must be made clear that social capital is a supplement, not an alternative, to organized efforts at the national level to address urban poverty and deprivation.

Social workers must keep these limitations in mind as they use social capital theory to promote local economic development. For this reason, they should not abandon their commitment to empowering and enhancing the political strengths of poor communities. However, the materialist perspective used in this article emphasizes the need to focus on economic development. This perspective is consistent with social work's commitment to serving the poor and oppressed. Indeed, improvements in the material welfare of the poor will increase their participation in civic associations, political action, and other forms of social capital that give them greater control over their lives.

REFERENCES

Balkin, S. (1989). *Self-employment for low-income people*. New York: Praeger.

Blakely, E. (1994). *Planning local economic development*. Thousand Oaks, CA: Sage Publications.

Coleman, J. (1988). Social capital in the creation of human capital, *American Journal of Sociology, 94*, 95-120.

Cox, F. (1995). Community problem solving: A guide to practice with comments. In J. Rothman, J. Ehrlich and J. Tropman (Eds.), *Strategies of community Intervention* (pp. 146-162). Itasca, IL: F. E. Peacock Publishers.

Dignard, L. & Havet, J. (Eds.), (1995). *Women in micro- and small-scale enterprise development*. Boulder, CO: Westview Press.

Else, J.F. & Raheim, S. (1992). AFDC clients as entrepreneurs: Self-employment offers an important option, *Public Welfare 50*, 36-41.

Etzioni, A. (1993). *The spirit of community: Rights, responsibilities and the communitarian agenda*. New York: Crown Publishers.

Fields, G.S. (1980). *Poverty, inequality and development*. New York: Cambridge University Press.

Fisher, R. (1994). *Let the people decide*. New York: Twayne Publishers.

Fukuyama, F. (1995). *Trust: The social virtues and the creation of prosperity*. New York: Free Press.

Granovetter, M.S. (1974). *Getting a job: A study of contacts and careers*. Cambridge, MA: Harvard University Press.

Livermore, M. (1996). Social work, social development and micro-enterprises:

Techniques and issues for implementation, *Journal of Applied Social Sciences, 21,* 37-44.

Midgley, J. (1995). *Social development: The developmental perspective in social welfare.* Thousand Oaks, CA: Sage Publications.

Midgley, J. (1996). Involving social work in economic development, *International Social Work, 39,* 13-27.

Midgley, J. & Simbi, P. (1993). Promoting a Developmental Focus in the Community Organization Curriculum: Relevance of the African Experience, *Journal of Social Work Education, 29,* 269-278.

National Association of Social Workers. (1995). *Encyclopedia of social work, 19th Edition.* Washington DC: NASW Press.

Netting, F., Kettner, P. & McMurtry, S. (1993). *Social work macro practice.* New York: Longman.

Psacharopoulos, G. (1973). *Returns to education: An international comparison.* Amsterdam: Elsevier.

Psacharopoulos, G. (1992) *Returns to investment to education: A global update.* Washington, DC: World Bank.

Putnum, R.D. with Leonardi, R. & Nanetti, R.Y. (1993). *Making democracy work: Civic traditions in modern Italy.* Princeton: Princeton University Press.

Putnum, R. (1995). Bowling alone: America's declining social capital, *Journal of Democracy, 6,* 65-78.

Putnum, R. (1996). The strange disappearance of civic America, *American Prospect,* Winter, 34-48.

Rothman, J. (1995). Approaches to community intervention. In J. Rothman, J. Ehrlich and J. Tropman (Eds.) *Strategies of community intervention* (pp. 26-63). Itasca, IL: F.E. Peacock Publishers.

Rubin, H. & Rubin, I. (1992). *Community organizing and development.* New York: Macmillan.

Sherraden, M. (1991). *Assets and the poor: A new American welfare policy.* Armonk, NY: M. E. Sharpe.

Skocpol, T. (1996). Unraveling from above, *The American Prospect, 25,* 20-25.

Thomas, K. (1994). *Community reinvestment performance: Making CRA work for banks, communities and regulators.* Chicago: Probus Publishing Company.

Wilson, W.J. (1987). *The truly disadvantaged: The inner city, the underclass and public policy.* Chicago: University of Chicago Press.

Self-Employment as a Social and Economic Development Intervention for Recipients of AFDC

Salome Raheim, PhD
Catherine F. Alter, PhD

SUMMARY. This paper reports findings from program evaluations of two demonstrations designed to (1) test self-employment as a social and economic development strategy for recipients of AFDC, and (2) identify policy barriers to improving the economic well-being of this population. The authors collected data through interviews with program participants and program operators and used secondary data contained in operators' management information systems and state Department of Human Services electronic files. Program results showed that self-employment is a viable social and economic development strategy for self-selected welfare recipients who receive business training and assistance in locating operating capital. The paper discusses implications for social work practice, education, and research. *[Article copies available for a fee from The Haworth Document Delivery Service: 1-800-342-9678. E-mail address: getinfo@haworthpressinc. com]*

With shrinking resources available to help poor families, community practitioners face the challenge of identifying interventions that both

Salome Raheim is Associate Professor at the School of Social Work, 308 North Hall, University of Iowa, Iowa City, IA 52242-1223 (e-mail: salome-raheim@uiowa.edu).

Catherine F. Alter is Dean of School of Social Work at the University of Denver.

[Haworth co-indexing entry note]: "Self-Employment as a Social and Economic Development Intervention for Recipients of AFDC." Raheim, Salome, and Catherine F. Alter. Co-published simultaneously in *Journal of Community Practice* (The Haworth Press, Inc.) Vol. 5, No. 1/2, 1998, pp. 41-61; and: *Community Economic Development and Social Work* (ed: Margaret S. Sherraden, and William A. Ninacs) The Haworth Press, Inc., 1998, pp. 41-61. Single or multiple copies of this article are available for a fee from The Haworth Document Delivery Service [1-800-342-9678, 9:00 a.m. - 5:00 p.m. (EST). E-mail address: getinfo@haworthpressinc.com].

empower these families and improve their economic well-being. An intervention to help poor families that has been all but invisible in the social work literature is self-employment development, sometimes called micro-enterprise development. While not the route out of poverty for all low-income people, self-employment is an important social and economic development strategy that merits the careful attention of community practitioners and other social workers.

This paper examines the background of self-employment development in the United States and reports outcome evaluations of two demonstration programs designed to (1) test self-employment as a social and economic development strategy for recipients of AFDC, and (2) identify policy barriers to improving the economic well-being of this population. The paper concludes with a discussion of the implications of these programs' findings for social work practice, education, and research in the areas of social and economic development.

BACKGROUND

Over the last two decades, job training and placement have gained considerable attention as welfare-to-work interventions. Lauded by some and severely criticized by others, these programs have been widely discussed in the social work literature (Bassi and Ashenfelter, 1986; Berg and Olson, 1991; Cloward and Piven, 1993; Gueron and Pauley, 1991; Hagen and Wang, 1994; Miller, 1990). By contrast, self-employment (also called micro-enterprise development) as an intervention strategy has received little attention in the social work literature. Yet despite the lack of academic attention, self-employment development programs for welfare recipients have gained the attention of policy makers. Results across the country are encouraging.

While microenterprise development appears to be a novel idea to many social workers, such programs have been implemented for many years in Africa, Latin America, Asia, and Europe with considerable success. In the United States, these programs have been developed during the last 10 years with promising results (Clark and Huston, 1993; Else and Raheim, 1992; Raheim, in press; Raheim and Alter, 1995; Raheim and Bolden, 1995). As early as 1986, the Demonstration Partnership Program of the Office of Community Service in the Department of Health and Human Services funded self-employment development demonstration projects for low-income people in New York and Vermont. Evaluations of these demonstration projects have indicated their effectiveness (U.S. Department of Health and Human Services, 1990). Subsequently, DHHS has approved or funded a variety of demonstrations across the nation to test micro-enterprise as a self-sufficiency strategy for welfare recipients and other low-income families (Guy, Doolittle, and Fink, 1991; U.S. Department of Health and Human Services, 1994).

Currently, more than 200 organizations in the United States operate self-employment development programs. These include community action agencies, community development corporations, women's organizations, refugee agencies, and single-purpose microenterprise groups. Seventy percent serve low-income and unemployed persons, while others target more specific groups such as women, Native Americans, AFDC recipients, displaced homemakers, dislocated workers, or Southeast Asian refugees (Clark, Huston, and Meister, 1994).

Self-employment development programs use a variety of approaches to promote microenterprise development. While these programs vary greatly, all offer one or more of the following components: (1) business training, (2) technical assistance, (3) lending, (4) assistance with securing financing from sources outside the program, and (5) family development and other counseling services.

Programs with a business training component provide micro-entrepreneurs with information and skills to successfully operate a business. Training focuses on business plan preparation, business management, self-esteem training, and personal financial management. Programs provide training in formal classroom settings or in internships. Most programs that provide training also offer on-going technical assistance for a specified period.

For participants who need to borrow start-up capital, microenterprise programs generally provide at least one of three options. Some programs provide loans directly to participants from their own loan pools. Others provide loans only through self-selected peer-lending groups. Peer lending is a model of financing developed by Mohammad Yunus and the Grameen Bank in Bangladesh–an innovative, government-owned, grass-roots-controlled bank organized specifically to encourage microenterprise by making small business loans (Yunus, 1988). Peer lending substitutes accountability to one's peers for collateral, since most low-income individuals have no assets to serve as collateral. A third program model helps participants secure commercial financing through helping them complete loan applications, coaching them in the presentation of their applications, and guaranteeing loans from the program's loan pool.

Along with business training or lending, some programs include a counseling or family development component (Raheim, 1995). These services help participants set personal and family goals and resolve circumstances that may hinder their success as entrepreneurs and impede their progress toward economic self-sufficiency.

Regardless of the diversity in the design of these programs, self-employment development is intended to achieve at least one of two purposes: economic development or economic self-sufficiency. Toward the end of economic development, these programs are intended to contribute to the economy by (1) creating jobs both for the entrepreneur and for additional employees, (2) encouraging innovation in the market place, and (3) stimulating economic activity. These programs are designed to help people get off of welfare by building their capacity to create jobs for themselves that will generate sufficient income to support their families.

The authors of this paper have conducted final evaluations of several self-employment programs for welfare recipients and other low-income people. This paper presents findings from evaluations of two of these programs: The Self-Employment Investment Demonstration (SEID) and the Rivercities of Iowa/Illinois Self-Employment Program (RISE).

TWO SELF-EMPLOYMENT DEMONSTRATION EVALUATIONS

The demonstrations discussed in this article were similar in design. One was implemented on a national level by several organizations, while the other was implemented in a bi-state area by a single organization. The Self-Employment Investment Demonstration (SEID) was the first national, publicly funded microenterprise program for low-income people in the United States. SEID was created to bring to the United States some of the benefits of microenterprise programs for low-income people that had been successfully implemented in other countries (Guy, Doolittle, and Fink, 1991). Specifically, SEID was designed to (1) test the viability of self-employment as a social and economic development strategy for AFDC recipients, and (2) remove the policy barriers that prevent AFDC recipients from becoming entrepreneurs, including income waivers to prevent reduction of participants' AFDC grants as a result of income generated during their first year of business operation. SEID implemented eight projects in five states–Iowa, Michigan, Minnesota, Mississippi, and Maryland–serving both urban and rural areas. Small business development centers, community colleges, a community action organization, and self-employment development organizations operated the projects. These organizations provided business training, technical assistance, and help in securing business loans. Some also provided individual loans, personal counseling, and other support services such as child care.

The Rivercities of Iowa/Illinois Self-Employment Program (RISE), implemented after SEID ended, served eight counties in an urban bi-state area. The non-profit organization that operated the Iowa SEID project also operated RISE and provided business training, technical assistance, and help in securing business loans. Together, the findings from the SEID and RISE evaluations document the potential social and economic impact of self-employment programs for low-income people, especially welfare recipients.

The SEID and RISE evaluations were similar in purpose and design. Each study measured two major outcomes: (1) the number and survival rate of businesses started through these projects, and (2) the impact of program participation on those who started businesses and their families, including subsequent levels of welfare receipt. We interviewed a random sample of program participants who started businesses for both studies.

The SEID and RISE evaluations differ in terms of methodologies used and types of data collected. The SEID evaluation is a follow-up study that examines participants' sources of income, assets, and perceptions of themselves and their quality of life before and after program participation. The RISE evaluation uses a pre- post-test design to measure changes in partici-pants' self-perceptions, as well as a comparison group to examine changes in welfare receipt. Each study makes a distinct contribution to understand-ing self-employment as a social and economic development strategy.

Self-Employment Investment Demonstration (SEID)

The University of Iowa, School of Social Work conducted the SEID post-program follow-up study in 1994. The study includes all SEID pro-grams except Maryland, since program implementation there began later than in the other states. The follow-up study identifies outcomes for a random sample of 120 SEID business owners, including the nature and size of their businesses, changes in family circumstances, and changes in economic self-sufficiency after starting their businesses.[1] The study con-centrates on participants who started new businesses in order to answer a central question of the demonstration: What happens to participants, their families, and their businesses after business start-up?

Interviews for the SEID evaluation elicited information about partici-pant outcomes by examining their family and financial circumstances before and after program participation. The schedules contained approxi-mately 200 open- and closed-ended items and took less than an hour to complete, on average. We analyzed the data using both quantitative and qualitative methods.

In the four states included in the follow-up study, 1,316 people partici-pated in SEID. Of these, 408 or 31% started businesses or strengthened their existing business through SEID participation. The typical SEID business owner was a white or African-American woman (46% and 35% respectively); a single head of household (68%); had two or fewer children (86%); had attended college (50%) or graduated from college (23%); and had received some vocational training (58%).

Financing of Business Start-Ups

SEID business owners used a variety of sources to finance their business starts or expansions. The three largest sources of financing for SEID businesses were the SEID programs themselves, personal funds, and commercial bank loans. SEID programs loaned an average of $5,605, banks loaned an average of $9,685, and personal funds (including funds generated by early business activities) averaged $3,009. Twenty-three percent of respondents had a loan guarantee from their SEID program operator for the commercial loans.

Characteristics of SEID Businesses

Most SEID businesses were sole proprietorships (n = 103, 86%). An additional 8% (n = 9) were jointly owned with a spouse. Seventy-two percent of all businesses in the sample were opened after enrollment in SEID, 20% were expansions of respondents' existing businesses, 4% were takeovers of existing businesses, and 2% were partnerships formed with existing businesses. Most businesses (73%) were in the service sector, while 20% were retail, 6% were manufacturing, and 1% was a wholesale business.

Business Survivals and Closures

The survival rates for SEID businesses exceed the national average for businesses of similar size, and support the contention that self-employment development programs can decrease failure rates among "disadvantaged" groups (Siegel, 1990; Weiss, 1990). Of the 120 businesses included in the SEID evaluation, 95 (79%) were still operating at the time of follow-up study. They had been in operation for an average of 2.6 years (31.5 months), and the range was from one month to eight years.

Of the 25 businesses (21%) in the sample that were no longer operating at the time of the interview, some closures were the result of positive outcomes, such as returning to school or accepting full-time employment. Other closures were the result of business failures due to insufficient business income, poor health, or difficult family circumstances. These businesses had operated for an average of 18.4 months, and their length of operation ranged from one month to five years.

Job Creation

In addition to the jobs SEID business owners created for themselves, they created 72 additional jobs–10 full-time, 54 part-time, and eight seasonal. Excluding the SEID business owner and the seasonal jobs, these businesses created an average of .53 jobs, approximately one new job for every two SEID businesses. In addition to existing jobs created, these businesses planned to make 30 additional hires within the 12 months following the survey.

Beyond the economic development benefit of the jobs created by SEID businesses, the program produced several non-economic benefits:

- 49 businesses employed family members at some time prior to the survey, including 21 of the respondents' children.
- 30 children of respondents had worked in these businesses on an unpaid basis, gaining employment experience.

1993 Business Assets and Liabilities

As a group, respondents had more business assets than liabilities. Respondents' business assets totaled $1,260,185 and included business property, materials, equipment, cars, and business checking accounts. Their liabilities totaled $677,150 and included mortgages on business property, business loans, car loans, and other debt. The total net worth for the group was $583,035. Average business assets were $10,921 and average liabilities was $5,739, leaving an average net worth of $5,182 per business.

Personal Assets

In addition to business assets, respondents had a number of personal assets at the time of the follow-up survey that they did not have when they enrolled in SEID. These assets included homes, cars, savings accounts, insurance policies, and other financial investments. The value of personal assets averaged $8,738 per participant. Because increasing assets is a critical factor in improving the well-being of low-income families (Sherraden, 1991), the dramatic increase in participants' business and personal assets indicates a meaningful improvement in the well-being of SEID participants and their families.

Reductions in AFDC and Food Stamps Receipt

AFDC and food stamps receipt was reduced among the sample of SEID participants who started businesses. The number of participants receiving AFDC benefits decreased by 50 percentage points, from 96.7% (n = 116) at the time of enrollment to 46.7% (n = 56) at the time of the interview, a statistically significant reduction (n = 120, X^2 = 58.02, p < .0001). Food stamps receipt decreased by 39.4 percentage points, from 91.2% (n = 104) to 51.8% (n = 59), a statistically significant reduction (n = 114, X^2 = 43.02, p < .0001).

Changes in Primary and Secondary Sources of Income

The distribution of primary and secondary sources of income for respondents shifted dramatically from the time of enrollment in SEID to the time of the follow-up study. Subsequent to SEID participation and starting a business, 55% of respondent families were producing their own primary source of income through their businesses or jobs, compared to only 9% who were doing so prior to SEID enrollment. Additionally, reliance on AFDC as a primary source of income declined from 74% to 26%, a decrease of 48 percentage points, and reliance on food stamps as a secondary source of income declined from 42% to 16%, a decrease of 26 percentage points. It is also interesting to note that a significant increase of 13% in the receipt of child support occurred, a possible indicator of increased empowerment of SEID participants.

Differences in Financial Stability

Most SEID participants' financial stability improved subsequent to SEID participation. A significant number of respondents were able to consistently buy food and clothing for their families after participation in SEID who had not been able to do so prior to enrollment. Further, participants reported that they were significantly more able to make timely personal loan and credit card payments.

Differences in Self-Esteem, Levels of Confidence and Quality of Life

Respondents were asked to evaluate the quality of several areas of their lives before and after participation in SEID.[2] Respondents reported significant improvements in the areas of income, relationships with spouses/ partners and children, and self-esteem. They reported their housing and health conditions as being the same (see Table 1). The only area in which they reported being worse off was personal time.

When asked to compare their lives and their feelings about themselves before they enrolled in SEID with the present, most respondents reported that their lives, their feelings about themselves, or their relationships with their families had improved in some way. Of the 114 respondents answering this item, most (n = 90) made at least one statement indicating more positive feelings, perceptions, or circumstances in their lives.

These respondents reported having more positive feelings and perceptions of themselves and their lives, such as being more self-confident, having more independence from family and others, and having greater self-esteem. One respondent said he could now see the "light at the end of

TABLE 1. Perceptions of Differences in Quality of Life Prior to SEID and Currently (N = 120)

	Better		Same		Worse	
	Number	%	Number	%	Number	%
Are you better, the same, or worse off in the following areas of your life now as compared with before your enrollment?						
Family income now vs. before	73	64.0%	30	26.3%	11	9.6%
Home now vs. before	43	38.4%	66	58.9%	3	2.7%
Relationship with child now vs. before	60	55.0%	46	42.2%	3	2.8%
Relationship with partner now vs. before	36	55.4%	25	38.5%	4	6.2%
Time for self now vs. before	33	29.7%	29	26.1%	49	44.1%
Health now vs. before	41	36.0%	51	44.7%	22	19.3%
Self-esteem now vs. before	86	76.1%	24	21.2%	3	2.7%

the tunnel." Another said that starting her own business had "given her a place in society and the community."

Of particular importance are participants' perceptions of increased self-efficacy (i.e., their abilities to influence their lives and achieve their goals). Examples of such statements are:

- "I believe that anything I set my mind to I can make it work; I believe that now. When people say I can't do it, I say that I can."
- "[My life] is more directed. I understand the steps I need to take to get where I'm going and get there successfully."
- "I feel better about myself, better self-esteem, more independent and motivated, and more positive about what I can do."
- "Before I got into the business, I was very depressed because of a lack of money to care for my children. Now it has totally changed and we have everything that we needed and want. [My family] seems to look up to me more now. I feel good about myself that I've accomplished all of these things. My kids are proud of me which is worth more than anything. People used to down grade me because I was on welfare. Now, I don't have that. I decided to set short goals for myself and have been able to accomplish them."

Respondents who indicated that their relationships with their families were better reported improvements such as more respect from family members and closer, less stressful family relationships. Some also reported feeling like a role model for their children, and that their children felt good about themselves.

Rivercities of Iowa/Illinois Self-Employment Program (RISE)

RISE was a three-year demonstration program that served eight counties in eastern Iowa and western Illinois. During the past decade, this region experienced serious economic problems, first during the farm crisis of the mid-1980s when all but one of the area's farm implement factories closed with a loss of 25,000 jobs, and then during the general Midwestern recession of the late 1980s. The area has not fully recovered from either of these events, and recovery has been slowed considerably by the horrendous floods of the summer of 1993.

We obtained the data for this evaluation from two sources. First, the program operator's management information system (MIS) provided a rich array of variables used for the process evaluation of the program. In addition, the Iowa Department of Human Service's electronic file contained grant records of all AFDC recipients for the prior five years. We compared RISE participants' movements toward self-sufficiency with those of a matched comparison group of AFDC recipients from a 14-county comparison region; these recipients had not participated in any welfare-to-work program except the state's JOBS program. We identified 61 matched pairs.[3]

Participant Characteristics

A total of 267 individuals enrolled in RISE. The typical RISE participant was white (72%), female (58%), a single parent (59%), had two children, had at least a high school diploma or GED (87%), and had some vocational training (50%). Additionally, 24% had technical certificates or college graduate degrees. Although most participants were white, the percent of participants of color (28%) were at least proportionate to their representation in the AFDC populations in the counties RISE served. Most RISE participants who were on welfare had been receiving AFDC for three and one-half years at the time of enrollment.

Program Results

The RISE logic model conceptualized the total program (training, assistance with securing financing, and on-going technical assistance) as having five milestones: (1) recruitment, (2) enrollment, (3) training completion, (4) business plan completion, (5) and business start-up. In addition, we specified two longer-term outcomes: (1) business survival for six months, and (2) business survival for one year. Table 2 summarizes comparisons of these planned objectives and the actual achievements of RISE.

As shown in Table 2, the RISE program exceeded each of its objectives, with variances that ranged from 112% in the case of the recruitment component to 198% in the case of the number of participants who finished their business plans. The program successfully assisted 76 low-income individuals in starting a business, exceeding the objectives by 141%.

Business Characteristics and Financing

Although most of the 76 RISE businesses (61%) were new, many (38%) were expansions of part-time, home-based businesses. Most businesses provided a service (70%), while the remainder were retail businesses (30%). Because participants were encouraged to pursue their own business ideas, consistent with their interests, skills, and experience, the products and services varied greatly. These businesses include automotive

TABLE 2. Process Results of RISE Program

Program Component	Expected[a]	Actual	Variance
Recruitment	500	559	112%
Enrollment	200	267	134%
Finished Training	180	216	120%
Finished Business Plan	80	158	198%
Started Business	54	76	141%
Six Months Survival	47	64	136%
One Year Survival	45	51	113%

[a]In the original proposal, the results projected for business starts and for six-month and for one-year survival were ranges; figures shown here are the midpoint of those ranges.

reconditioning, catering, computer services, pest control, house painting, quilting, professional resume writing, and floor tile and carpet installation.

RISE businesses received a total of $203,400 in financing, primarily from commercial banks (67%), since the program did not provide direct loans to participants. Other sources of financing included churches (11%), government loans such as a state loan for low-income entrepreneurs (14%), and private sources such as family and friends (6%).

Business Survival Rate

Of the 76 original RISE businesses, 67% were still open one year after starting or expanding through the program. Of the 33% that closed, eight (11%) businesses were sold, including one that merged with another business and two whose owners subsequently started another business. Thus, it is important to note that business closure and business failure are not synonymous. The circumstances of some business closures indicate positive outcomes.

The major question asked by policy makers is whether self-employment development programs like RISE can enable AFDC recipients to move off welfare more quickly than more traditional welfare-to-work programs. The RISE evaluation attempted to answer this question in two ways.

First, we found that 68.9% of RISE participants and 45.9% of the comparison group had exited AFDC within the first year after the enrollment date. Likewise, more than 90% of RISE participants had exited

AFDC within two years after enrollment, as compared with 83.6% of the comparison group. Only 1.6% of RISE participants were still on AFDC after 30 months as compared with 6.9% of non-participants. These were statistically significant differences.

The challenge in relying solely on this approach to answer the outcome question is that almost half of all of the individuals in both groups who exited AFDC sometime after the beginning of the study had returned to AFDC before the end of the study, September 30, 1993. Thus, it seems that using the first exit date creates an unrealistic impression of the performance of one group or both groups. For this reason, we took a second approach to analyzing the data.

Table 3 displays three variables. The first is the average maximum months that study participants could have been on AFDC during the study period. Individuals enrolled in one of 19 training cycles over almost a three-year period. Thus, the number of months ranged from one to 31 months. This variable is included in the table to demonstrate that the

TABLE 3. Average Percent of Months Two Groups Were Off AFDC Between Their Enrollment Date and September 30, 1993.

	RISE (N = 61)	Comparison (N = 61)
Average Maximum Number of Months Recipients Could Have Been on AFDC Between Their Enrollment and Sept. 30, 1993	17.528	17.523
Average Actual Number of Months Recipients Received AFDC Benefits Between Their Enrollment and Sept. 30, 1993	12.607	15.984
Average Percent of Months Recipients were OFF AFDC During the Period of Time They Could Have Been ON AFDC[a]	.252	.072

[a]Analysis of Variance indicates there was a statistically significant difference between the mean number of months the RISE group was off AFDC as compared with the mean number of months for the comparison group during the study period ($F = 7.94$; $p = .0005$).

matching process was successful and, on average, the groups had an equal amount of time to move toward self-sufficiency. Not only are the mean number of months almost identical, but so are the standard deviations (RISE Std. Dev. = 9.152; and comparison Std. Dev. = 9.227).

The second variable is the average actual number of months that each group received an AFDC check during the period between participant's enrollment month and September, 1993. As Table 3 shows, the RISE group averaged 12.61 months of AFDC receipt (Std. Dev. = 9.0 months), and the comparison group averaged 15.98 months (Std. Dev. = 8.9 months).

The third variable is the average percent of months in which participants/recipients did not receive AFDC benefits as a proportion of the time they could have received benefits.[4] The RISE group was off of AFDC for an average of 25% of the time (Std. Dev. = .314), while the comparison group was off of AFDC for an average of 7.2% of the time (Std. Dev. = .167). This is a statistically significant difference. The recipients in RISE spent more time off of AFDC than the comparison group.

To measure the impact of training and business start-up, we asked RISE participants to complete a set of questionnaires at three data collection points during the program: enrollment, training completion, and business start-up or three months after training completion. To measure changes in participants' self-esteem, we used the Index of Self-Esteem (ISE) because of its ease of administration, reliability, and validity (Hudson, 1990). The ISE is a 25-item measure of the degree or magnitude of problems participants have with their self-esteem or sense of self-worth. Table 4 shows the results of the ISE at three times during the course of the RISE program.

As shown in Table 4, there was a small, but statistically significant increase in participants' self-esteem as they experienced the RISE program. At the baseline measurement point, the scores were 90+; at later points, the scores had generally risen above 100. For participants who started a business, as well as those who did not, there was a steady improvement in the way participants perceived themselves (F = 7.2; p = .001).

To measure changes in skills relevant to economic self-sufficiency, participants completed the Time and Money Management Skills (TMM) questionnaire. The TMM is a 15-item, five-point semantic differential scale that assesses an individual's (1) effective planning and control of time, energy, and financial resources; and (2) successful allocation of resources in the areas of health, quality of life, and indebtedness. The average TMM scores for the group of participants who started businesses, as well as the group that did not, improved over time. At enrollment, the scores were 30+ compared to 50+ at business start-up (or three months after training completion for those who did not start a business), a signifi-

TABLE 4. Repeated Measures of Participants' Perceptions of Their Self-Esteem RISE Demonstration, Oct. 1,1990-Sept. 30, 1993

	Mean	Std. Dev.	Std. Err.
Baseline (Enrollment) Did not start business (N = 33) Did start business (N = 42)	92.1 93.7	23.3 23.2	4.1 3.6
Time 1 (Finish Training) Did not start business (N = 33) Did start business (N = 42)	100.1 99.1	13.7 19.7	2.4 3.0
Time 2 (Start-Up) Did not start business (N = 33) Did start business (N = 42)	101.6 100.7	12.9 15.2	2.3 2.3
F-Value	7.2		
p-Value	.001		

cant increase ($F = 33.9$; $p < .001$). This finding suggests that the training improved participants' perceptions of self-efficacy regarding their ability to control their personal and financial resources. Table 5 presents TMM questionnaire results.

DISCUSSION

Together, the findings of the SEID and RISE evaluations provide important information about self-employment development with people who receive welfare, including (1) who pursues this self-sufficiency option, (2) what are the survival rates of the businesses they operate, (3) what reductions in welfare receipt are possible, and (4) what are the effects of program participation and business ownership.

The characteristics of those who pursued self-employment as a route off of welfare were similar in some ways to others receiving AFDC, but dissimilar in others. Like other AFDC recipients, most were female single heads of household. The racial-ethnic composition of participants groups was proportionate to their representation in local AFDC populations. However, they were older and more likely to have graduated from high

TABLE 5. Repeated Measures of Participants' Time and Money Management

	Mean	Std. Dev.	Std. Err.
Baseline (Enrollment) Did not start business (N = 33) Did start business (N = 42)	38.3 34.2	25.3 25.5	4.3 3.9
Time 1 (Finish Training) Did not start business (N = 33) Did start business (N = 42)	39.3 34.8	24.3 24.5	4.1 3.7
Time 2 (Start-Up) Did not start business (N = 33) Did start business (N = 42)	55.1 53.8	10.7 9.2	1.8 1.4
F-Value	33.9		
p-Value	< .0001		

school, hold a GED, or to have completed some college or vocational training than is typical among AFDC populations. The differences between participants in these programs and others on AFDC are consistent with the Institute for Women's Policy Research comparison of self-employed, current and former welfare recipients with other women on welfare (Spalter-Roth, Soto, and Zandniapour, 1994).

While the percentages of African-Americans in SEID and RISE were proportionate to their numbers in the local AFDC populations, this percentage is much higher than the proportion of African American business owners in the general population. These findings suggest that self-employment development programs like those discussed here can decrease barriers and increase opportunities for business ownership among economically disadvantaged African-Americans.

Almost all of the businesses started through these programs are sole proprietorships or jointly owned by couples. The recruitment and training approaches used in these types of programs encourage the development of sole proprietorship businesses. Participants are recruited individually through information sent with public assistance checks, public service announcements, or notices posted in the community. Programs focus on teaching individuals how to create their own businesses. This approach contrasts with other economic development strategies, such as the establishment of community cooperatives and worker ownership, which involve entrepreneurs working together as groups (Bendick and Egan, 1995).

The survival rate of SEID businesses (79%) was somewhat higher than that of RISE businesses (67%). Since no correlations were found between business closure and a variety of variables (e.g., type of business, participant age, education, marital status, number of children), we assume that other, unidentified variables are related to business closure, such as local economic conditions. The lower survival rates found among RISE businesses may be related to the slow recovery from the farm crisis, the general Midwestern recession of the mid-1980s, and the Flood of 1993. Since SEID findings represent businesses from a variety of geographic regions, we assume that SEID findings are more representative of the potential survival rate of businesses started with the assistance of these types of programs. The findings indicate the need for further research to identify factors associated with business survival and failure.

Both SEID and RISE findings document that self-employment programs can reduce welfare receipt. RISE findings show that participants spent less time on welfare than those in a matched comparison group who were participating in a traditional welfare-to-work program.

Beyond welfare savings, SEID and RISE produced important social and economic development effects. These programs increased people's capacity to create employment for themselves by providing access to the knowledge, skills, and capital needed. Program participants were empowered to assume new roles in the economy of their communities. Further, the business and personal asset accumulation and the job creation by these businesses are economic development benefits that are specific to microenterprise development.

Two types of non-economic outcomes of these programs merit attention. One is changes in participants' self-perceptions. Although the SEID and RISE studies used different methodologies to assess changes in self-efficacy and self-esteem, both studies found that these attributes increased subsequent to program participation. The combined findings of these studies suggest that program participation improves participants' self-perceptions, whether or not they start a business.

The other non-economic outcome is the effect of employing family members, especially children. Both studies found that businesses in these demonstrations employed family members, including a substantial number of children. It is reasonable to hypothesize that the experience of working in a family-owned business may have important social and psychological benefits for the children of welfare recipients and other family members, including increases in self-esteem, self-efficacy, and future economic self-sufficiency. This issue merits exploration in future studies of families that engage in self-employment as a route off of welfare.

The pattern of financing for SEID and RISE businesses has important implications for economic development. Consistent with the findings of microenterprise development studies abroad (Ashe, 1985; Grindle, Mann, and Shipton, 1987), our findings demonstrate that intermediaries, such as SEID and RISE program operators, played a central role in helping participants develop relationships with banks and influencing banks to make loans to participants, who usually had poor credit histories and no collateral. These findings also demonstrate that banks can play an important role in financing businesses of low-income people. They are encouraged to do so through the Community Reinvestment Act of 1977, which requires regulated financial institutions to help meet the credit needs of their local communities.

IMPLICATIONS FOR SOCIAL AND ECONOMIC DEVELOPMENT AND SOCIAL WORK

Research has shown that about 5% percent of people receiving welfare are likely to use self-employment, concurrently, as a way to improve their families' economic well-being (Spalter-Roth, Soto, and Zandniapour, 1994). Findings from the SEID and RISE demonstrations document that self-employment development with welfare recipients and other low-income people has both social and economic development benefits. The challenge for the social work profession is to use these findings to inform practice, education, and research. There are several ways that the profession can meet this challenge.

First, we must re-examine our perception of economic development. Many practitioners view economic development only as a top-down macro planning strategy, which is neither relevant to individual and community empowerment nor within the domain of social work. Contrary to this view, self-employment development can be an empowering, bottom-up development strategy that falls squarely within social work's mission. It builds human capital while helping the poor to improve their material conditions. Midgley and Simbi (1993) remind us of the importance of using development strategies that go beyond mobilizing to improve the material well-being of those we serve.

Second, social workers can use the findings of micro-enterprise development studies to inform policy practice. Self-employment is a successful development strategy for members of poor communities when (1) intermediary organizations are present to provide the knowledge, skills, and access to capital; and (2) welfare policy barriers to income generation and asset building are removed (Raheim and Alter, 1995). Advocacy is needed to support self-employment development organizations and to remove policy barriers that would prevent welfare recipients from pursuing self-employment.

Third, social work curricula would be enhanced by including self-employment as a social and economic development intervention. Midgley and Simbi (1993) discuss the importance of integrating such interventions in social work curricula, for example, in the presentation of community development strategies. Case studies of micro-enterprise development would provide social work students with an opportunity to learn an intervention that directly provides low-income individuals with the tools and supports to improve their economic well-being through income generation and asset building. Additionally, micro-enterprise development organizations could provide important experiences for students in practice.

Fourth, social work research in self-employment development programs would build our knowledge base regarding various dimensions of social and economic development. Among the questions that could be explored are: How does working in a family-owned business affect the children of welfare recipients? Can self-employment development organizations help communities implement other economic development strategies, such as consortia and cooperatives? How do self-employment development programs affect poor communities? There is much to learn about self-employment as an intervention for the poor, and social worker researchers could make significant contributions.

Finally, social workers must be careful not to overstate the benefits of these programs. Because experimental designs are rarely used in these programs and participant self-selection is central to this intervention, program findings cannot be generalized to the broader AFDC population. However, they may be generalizable to those individuals who will voluntarily enroll in self-employment development programs. These individuals are predisposed to self-employment and business ownership to the extent that they will pursue self-employment training when programs designed for them are available.

We must be careful not to create an Horatio Alger myth about entrepreneurial programs for welfare recipients. While this intervention is effective for a small but significant number of people who have the necessary interest to become self-employed, it is not a broad solution to poverty. To eliminate poverty, we need a comprehensive process of economic development (Midgley, 1995). Micro-enterprise development can create economic opportunity for the poor and assist low-income families to improve their economic well-being.

REFERENCES

Ashe, Je. (1985*). The PISCES II Experience: Local Efforts in Micro-Enterprise Development*. Volume I. Washington, DC: Agency for International Development.

Bassi, L.J., & Ashenfelter, O. (1986). The effect of direct job creation and training programs on low-skilled workers. In S.H. Danziger & D.H. Weinberg (Eds.), *Fighting poverty: What works and what doesn't* (pp. 133-151). Cambridge, MA: Harvard University Press.

Berg, L., & Olson, L. (1991). *Causes and implications of rapid job loss among participants in a welfare to work program*. Paper presented at the Annual Research Conference of the Association for Public Policy and Management, Bethesda, MD.

Bendick, J.M., & Egan, M.L. (1995). Worker ownership and participation enhances economic development in low-opportunity communities. *Journal of Community Practice, 2*(1), 61-85.

Clark, M., & Huston, T. (1993). *Assisting the smallest business: Assisting micro-enterprise development as a strategy for boosting poor communities. An interim report*. Washington, DC: Self-Employment Learning Project, Aspen Institute.

Clark, M., Huston, T., & Meister, B. (1994). *1994 Directory of Micro-Enterprise Programs*. Washington, DC: Self-Employment Learning Project, Aspen Institute for Humanistic Studies.

Cloward, R.A., & Piven, F.F. (1993, June). The fraud of workfare. *The Nation,* 693-696.

Else, J.F., & Raheim, S. (1992). AFDC clients as entrepreneurs: Self-employment offers an important option. *Public Welfare, 50*(4), 36-41.

Grindle, M.S., Mann, C. K., & Shipton, P.M. (1987). *ARIES (Assistance to Resource Institutions for Enterprise Support): Capacity Building for Resource Institutions for Small and Micro-Enterprises–A Strategic Overview Paper*. Prepared by the Harvard Institute for International Development for the Office of Rural and Institutional Development Bureau for Science and Technology and Office of Private and Voluntary Cooperation, Bureau of Food for Peace and Voluntary Assistance, U.S. Agency for International Development, Washington, DC 20523, Contract Number DAN-1090-C-00-5124-00.

Gueron, J.M. & Pauley, E. (1991). *From welfare to work*. New York: Russell Sage.

Guy, C., Doolittle, F., & Fink, B.L. (1991). *Self-employment for welfare recipients: Implementation of the SEID program*. New York: Manpower Demonstration Research Corporation.

Hagen, J.L., & Wang, L. (1994). Implementing JOBS: The functions of frontline workers. *Social Service Review,* June, 369-385.

Hudson, W.W. (1990). *WALMYR Assessment Scale scoring manual*. Tempe, AZ: WALMYR Publishing Co.

Midgley, J. (1995). *Social development: The developmental perspective in social welfare*. Thousand Oaks, CA: Sage Publications.

Midgley, J., & Simbi, P. (1993). Promoting a development focus in the community organization curriculum: Relevance of the African experience. *Journal of Social Work Education, 29*(3), 269-278.

Miller, D.C. (1990). *Women and social welfare: A feminist analysis.* New York: Praeger.

Raheim, S. (in press). Micro-enterprise as an approach for promoting economic development in social work: Lessons from the Self-Employment Investment Demonstration. *International Social Work.*

Raheim, S. (1995). Self-employment training and family development: An integrated strategy for family empowerment, pp. 127-143. In K. Nelson & P. Adams (Eds.), *Reinventing human services.* Hawthorne, New York: Aldine de Gruyter.

Raheim, S., & Alter, C. F. (1995). *Final evaluation report: The Self-Employment Investment Demonstration.* Washington, DC: Corporation for Enterprise Development.

Raheim, S., & Bolden, J. (1995). Economic empowerment of low-income women through self-employment. *Affilia, 10*(2), 138-154.

Sherraden, M. (1991). *Assets and the poor: A new American welfare.* Armonk, New York: M. E. Sharpe.

Siegel, B. (1990). Business creation and local economic development: Why entrepreneurship should be encouraged. In *Local initiative for job creation: Enterprising women* (pp. 85-99). Paris: Organisation for Economic Co-operation and Development.

Spalter-Roth, R., Soto, E., & Zandniapour, L. (with J. Braunstein). (1994). *Microenterprise and women: The viability of self-employment as a strategy for alleviating poverty.* Washington DC: Institute for Women's Policy Research.

U.S. Department of Health and Human Services, Administration for Children and Families, Office of Community Services. (1994). *Demonstration Partnership Program Projects: Micro Business and Self-Employment, Summary of Final Evaluation Findings from 1990.* Monograph Series 200-90, Contract Number: HHS-105-92-8204. Washington, DC: Author.

U.S. Department of Health and Human Services, Office of Community Services, Family Support Administration. (1990). *Demonstration Partnership Program: Summary and Findings, FY 1987 Demonstration Partnership Program Projects.* Washington, DC: Author.

Weiss, C. (1990). The role of intermediaries in strengthening women's self-employment activities. In *Local initiative for job creation: Enterprising women* (pp. 59-74). Paris: Organisation for Economic Co-operation and Development.

Yunus, M. (1988). *Grameen Bank: Organization and operations.* Prepared for the Microenterprise Conference, U.S. Agency for International Development. Washington, DC: Author.

Micro-Enterprise Development:
A Response to Poverty

Mahasweta M. Banerjee, PhD

SUMMARY. All over the world, micro-enterprise development initiatives are demonstrating that they are a viable response to poverty. This paper discusses a field study of 40 slum-dwellers, 17 of whom had taken out a loan for a micro-enterprise, conducted in Calcutta in 1995. This study helps demonstrate the crucial elements of the Grameen model of micro-lending. Findings show there is a significant difference in income of borrowers versus non-borrowers, and that micro-enterprises create a culture that has rippling effects on the community. Lessons learned are relevant for social workers promoting micro-enterprises for community economic development in the United States. *[Article copies available for a fee from The Haworth Document Delivery Service: 1-800-342-9678. E-mail address: getinfo@haworthpressinc. com]*

A micro-enterprise, true to its meaning, is a very small business operated by a low-income individual with a loan. All over the world, micro-enterprise development projects demonstrate that small businesses such as designer dress shops, desktop publishing companies, flower shops, recycl-

---

Mahasweta M. Banerjee is Assistant Professor, School of Social Welfare, University of Kansas, Lawrence, KS 66045 (e-mail: mahaswetab@sw1.socwel. ukans.edu).

The author is grateful to the School of Social Welfare, University of Kansas, Lawrence, Kansas for a Junior Faculty Grant to study "The Interplay of Strengths and Constraints in the Life of Slum Dwellers in Calcutta," in the summer of 1995.

[Haworth co-indexing entry note]: "Micro-Enterprise Development: A Response to Poverty." Banerjee, Mahasweta M. Co-published simultaneously in *Journal of Community Practice* (The Haworth Press, Inc.) Vol. 5, No. 1/2, 1998, pp. 63-83; and: *Community Economic Development and Social Work* (ed: Margaret S. Sherraden, and William A. Ninacs) The Haworth Press, Inc., 1998, pp. 63-83. Single or multiple copies of this article are available for a fee from The Haworth Document Delivery Service [1-800-342-9678, 9:00 a.m. - 5:00 p.m. (EST). E-mail address: getinfo@haworthpressinc.com].

63

ing services, and grocery stores allow low-income individuals to gain economic self-sufficiency. Sometimes, they generate savings and home ownership and create employment opportunities for others. Additionally, there are numerous psycho-social and political benefits of micro-enterprise ownership, such as confidence, dignity, family stability, and empowerment. Thus, micro-enterprise development projects are increasingly considered a viable anti-poverty strategy (Bornstein, 1996; Counts, 1996; Holcombe, 1995; Raheim, 1996; Solomon, 1992; Yunus, 1995; 1990; 1987).

Social work has a long, albeit piecemeal, history with community building (Weil and Gamble, 1995). Micro-enterprise development is a promising new approach for social workers to help impoverished communities revive themselves. Not only do micro-enterprises provide an empowering choice to many individuals whose other alternatives are unemployment or low-wage, dead-end jobs, but also they hold the potential of revitalizing local economies by catering services and products needed locally, thereby rebuilding communities from within. Thus, micro-enterprises are a powerful move against the face of seemingly intractable poverty in disintegrating communities. Throughout the world, social workers endeavoring to mitigate poverty can combine micro-meso and macro strategies with micro-enterprise development initiatives to build more self-sufficient communities.

The Grameen Bank's phenomenal success with micro-lending which enabled very poor women in Bangladesh to start small businesses and earn livings reverberates throughout much of the globe. This paper will report on a study of micro-enterprise development in India that adapted Bangladesh's Grameen model and draws lessons from this study for the United States. Because three countries are involved, this paper will first review and critique micro-enterprise development programs in Bangladesh, India, and the United States. Next, the paper will present the field study in which the crucial elements of the Grameen model are first presented, followed by an examination of the impact of the micro-enterprise program on 40 residents of a slum in Calcutta, India. The study will show that among the 40 residents studied, 17 who had taken out loans for micro-enterprises had significantly higher incomes than the non-borrowers and that micro-enterprises created a culture that had rippling effects on the community. Last, the paper will discuss lessons from this study and draw implications for social workers promoting and implementing micro-enterprises for community economic development in the United States.

MICRO-ENTERPRISE DEVELOPMENT PROGRAMS
IN BANGLADESH, INDIA, AND THE UNITED STATES

Since the 1970s, micro-enterprise development programs have been operating in developing nations like Latin America and Africa (Ashe, 1985; Baydas, Meyer, and Aguilera-Alfred, 1994; de Soto, 1989; Morewagae, Rempel, and Seemule, 1995), and developed nations like France and Britain (Balkin, 1989; Puls, 1988; Raheim, 1996). More recently, they have been implemented in Southeast Asian countries (Kamaluddin, 1993; Tyler, 1995; *WIN News,* 1995), as well as in Norway and Canada (Counts, 1996; Margolis, 1996).

Developed and developing nations have many differences. Only two differences, among many, are their welfare programs and their agricultural sectors. A major difference between American welfare programs and those in India and Bangladesh, is that the latter two countries do not have any income maintenance programs, though free health care and primary education are available to all. Consequently, poor people must find a way to make a living to survive. Unlike the United States, both India and Bangladesh have large agricultural sectors with poverty rates higher in rural than in urban areas (Dutta, 1996; Rahman and Wahid, 1992). For these reasons, micro-enterprise development programs in Bangladesh and India were originally designed to address rural poverty.

Bangladesh. Grameen, translated into English, means rural. However, the Grameen Bank is much more than a mere rural bank; it is a poverty alleviation program and community development movement. The paper presents the program's poverty alleviation aspects in this section; it will discuss its operational mechanisms as well as community developmental aspects in the research section.

After seven years of experimenting with various micro-lending strategies with poor rural people, economist Muhammad Yunus established the Grameen Bank in 1983. His goal was to demonstrate that poor people can generate enough income from micro-enterprises to support small-scale lending through a formal bank. Yunus (1995; 1990) believes that credit is a fundamental human right and that women borrowers are better credit risks than men. Thus, more than 92% of Grameen's borrowers are women (Holloway and Wallich, 1992). In May 1994, the Grameen Bank had 1,915,000 borrower members, who started micro-enterprises in 34,243 villages of Bangladesh, served by 1,042 Grameen Bank branches (Holcombe, 1995). The beneficiary population increases to around ten million if one assumes that the benefits of credit and savings reach the whole family of five or six people. Holcombe (1995) noted that by May 1994, cumulative loan disbursement exceeded $1 billion U.S. and unpaid loans after two years were at an enviable level of 1.32%; almost 99% of the member borrowers had returned their loans on time, which allowed the money to be reused for additional loans.

The First Lady of the United States, Hillary Rodham Clinton, visited Bangladesh in 1995 and lauded the successes of the Grameen Bank in addressing the plight of poor rural women. The media coverage on Hillary Clinton's visit drew America's attention to the Grameen Bank's significant impact on social, economic, and political aspects of poor rural women's lives (Klein, 1995). From a purely economic point of view, the loans enabled poor, illiterate, rural women in one of the poorest nations in the world, Bangladesh, to make a living through micro-enterprises (Bornstein, 1996; Counts, 1996; Holcombe, 1995; Solomon, 1992). In a study of five Grameen villages, Hossain (1988) found that Grameen Bank households' income was 43% higher than target group households in control villages and 28% higher than those of non-participants in Grameen villages. Further, income increase was greatest for the absolutely landless and for the marginal landowners, and micro-enterprises generated new employment. A 1993 study found that 46% of women who had borrowed for eight years or more had crossed the poverty line, as opposed to 4% of non-borrowers; another 34% had increased their income but were still poor, while the remaining 20% remained mired in extreme poverty (Bornstein, 1996).

Hossain (1988) also found that although borrowers initially invested in agricultural and non-agricultural production, after three years, they tended to put their money in social investment, housing, education, and sanitation. Thus, some women were able to save money and received additional loans to buy homes in their own names. This had socio-political consequences because the power and status of women improved significantly. Marriage became more stable for these women as Muslim men, allowed to marry four wives, remained faithful to one because of the stability provided by her income and her home. Holcombe (1995) reported a study with 120 women that found that their husbands treated them more equally, while physical violence and verbal abuse decreased. Moreover, since women were now in charge of the money, they spent it on food for their children. This improved children's health and nutrition and some were able to attend school rather than work. In short, the Grameen Bank's credit management program for developing micro-enterprises is, overall, a great national success (Bornstein, 1996; Counts, 1996; Holcombe, 1995; Solomon, 1992).

Despite its successes in addressing poverty, the Grameen model has critics. They claim that micro-enterprises financed by the Grameen Bank result in only marginal improvements in the lives of very poor, illiterate women. Moreover, these women experience tremendous pressure to repay loans on time, with the standard 16% annual interest. Jain (1996) determined that the acclaimed policy of replacing individual collateral with group guarantee is not always practiced; rather, the program's success is due to shaping borrowers' and Bank personnel's behavior through the creation of an organizational culture. Some (Holloway and Wallich, 1992; Kamaluddin, 1993; Tameen, 1990) question the profitability and sustainability of the Grameen Bank and argue that it is only able to break even because of substantial subsidies. It still remains to be seen whether the Grameen Bank is commercially viable.

India. The voluntary social service sector implemented micro-enterprise programs in rural India as far back as the 1970s, encouraging poor rural people to start goat rearing businesses, cattle and fish farming, and so on. However, these programs were outright grants, not loans to be repaid with interest. These sporadic measures enabled a few to survive, but did not have any significant impact on widespread and deep-rooted rural poverty.

The Self-Employed Women's Association (SEWA), a non-governmental agency, registered a cooperative bank in 1974 to bridge the gap between commercial banks and illiterate, slum-dwelling women. These women received credit to start a micro-enterprise. At the end of 1989, SEWA had 25,000 clients and by 1992, when it opened branches in rural areas, the clientele had doubled to 50,000 (Spodek, 1994). However, SEWA's main focus is not on individual micro-enterprise development; rather, it concentrates on developing unions and women's cooperatives for dairy farming, wool and cotton-weaving, and handicrafts (Rose, 1992).

During 1980-1985, the Indian federal government started extending small scale loans to villagers for starting micro-enterprises through the Integrated Rural Development Programme (IRDP). Bandyopadhyay (1985) states, "The core of the IRDP philosophy is the endowment of income generating asset to the assetless" (p. 121). This means-tested subsidized interest program reached more than 15 million rural families within a five-year period and charged a 10.25% interest; loan recovery rate was 69% (Bandyopadhyay, 1989). Various evaluation studies of the IRDP (Institute for Financial Management and Research, 1984; Reserve Bank of India, 1984; National Bank for Agriculture and Rural Development, 1984; Programme Evaluation Organization, 1985) reported that 37% to 49% of eligible borrowers moved above the official poverty line and 51% to 88% of sample households received incremental income. Further, the IFMR study reported that 84% felt subjectively "happy" or "very happy" with the program. On the other hand, Dutta (1996) noted that all of the federal guaranteed wage employment schemes combined, including the National Rural Employment Programme and the Rural Landless Employment

Guarantee Programme, provided jobs for less than 10% of unemployed rural people. Thus, a comparison of these two income-generating schemes suggests that micro-lending is more effective than guaranteed wage employment in addressing rural poverty. Nevertheless, despite some measurable successes, the IRDP program has been solidly criticized for mismanagement of funds, for not reaching the poorest of the poor, for resembling more of an outright grant than a loan to be repaid with interest, and for not reaching poor women (Bandyopadhyay, 1985; 1989; Dutta, 1996).

Although 35% of India's urban population live below the poverty line (Dutta, 1996), the Indian government does not have any micro-lending program for micro-enterprise development in urban areas; only those with collateral can borrow from commercial banks. The voluntary social service sector addresses the need for loans by running micro-enterprise programs in urban India (*WIN news,* 1995). However, hardly any literature is available on urban micro-enterprise programs in India.

The United States. The political-economic reality of the 1980s led private agencies and segments of public sector agencies to develop micro-enterprise development initiatives in the United States. In 1996, more than 300 micro-enterprise development programs were operating in the United States (Clark, Huston, and Meister, 1994). Some are run by women's organizations supported by private funding, others are community action agencies using public dollars. Some serve women of all economic levels, others serve only low-income women, while still others serve all low-income citizens. Some require collateral, most charge interest, and a few follow the Grameen model.

Connie Evans (1996), Director of Women's Self-Employment Project (WSEP) based in Chicago and incorporated in 1986, reported that Aspen Institute's evaluation of WSEP found that the program was successful in helping the most disadvantaged women move toward economic self-sufficiency by providing them with training and credit. The study found that, over a three-year period, 25% of the women got out of poverty because of their micro-enterprises, 80% were operating their micro-enterprises after three years, 60% of respondents' net worth increased, and two-thirds of the micro-enterprises employed staff and paid $6 an hour to as many as four employees. Further, the WSEP adapted the Grameen model of lending that Counts (1996) and Solomon (1992) discuss in great detail.

Also in 1986, the Self-Employment Investment Demonstration (SEID) launched a national micro-enterprise demonstration project targeted toward AFDC recipients in Iowa, Maryland, Michigan, Minnesota, and Mississippi. Raheim (1996) conducted a study of 120 SEID participants and found that the program had both economic and psycho-social benefits.

She found that: (a) 60% of women terminated their AFDC benefits; (b) mean reported business income was $21,231; (c) some women acquired personal assets; (d) participants had more business assets than liabilities; (e) 79% of businesses were operating for an average of 2.6 years; (f) some businesses created new jobs; and (g) participants reported a significant increase in confidence, self-esteem, and control over their future. Thus, various evaluations of micro-enterprise programs in the United States indicate that they are a viable economic option for some low-income women when welfare policy barriers are removed and supports are provided (Edgcomb, Klein and Clark, 1996; Evans, 1996; Raheim, 1997; 1996; Spalter-Roth, Soto and Zandniapour, 1994; Solomon, 1992).

The studies reviewed suggest various similarities and differences in micro-enterprise development programs in Bangladesh, India, and the United States. Comparing the micro-enterprise development initiatives of Bangladesh and India, it is clear that although the IRDP program has reached more people, the Grameen program has greater success in loan repayment. A key to Bangladesh's higher repayment rate is the creation of solidarity groups, which are not required by India's IRDP program. On the other hand, some voluntary sector programs in both the United States and India follow the Grameen model of micro-lending through groups. Unlike Bangladesh, public and some private programs in India as well as some private programs in the United States do not have a gender preference. Future studies in other countries should examine the validity of the Grameen model's gender preference in micro-lending. Moreover, there are numerous policy barriers against micro-enterprise development in the United States such as income and asset limits (see Raheim, 1997; Solomon, 1992 for details), but not in Bangladesh and India. Last, low-income individuals in all three countries benefit from skills training, developing business plans, marketing and pricing, and accessing social supports. In conclusion, despite a few differences, the common denominator is that micro-enterprises enable some people to become economically self-sufficient in all three countries.

THE GRAMEEN MODEL APPLIED IN A CALCUTTA SLUM

To get first hand knowledge about the Grameen model, I visited a particular slum in Calcutta during the summer of 1995. The purpose of this field study was to inquire into: (a) how and why the Grameen model of micro-enterprise development works; (b) whether the Grameen model of micro-enterprise development works in an urban setting of a different country; and (c) what is the socio-economic impact of a micro-enterprise program on poor people living in an impoverished community.

Methodology. The data analyzed in this paper comprise one component of a larger qualitative study designed to explore the interplay of strengths and constraints in the life of slum dwellers in Calcutta. Dhobiatalla became the study site because it was the only slum in Calcutta where the Institute for Motivating Self-Employment (IMSE), a non-governmental social service agency and pioneer in micro-enterprise development in rural Eastern India, operated its credit management program.

From mid-June till the end of July 1995, I interviewed 40 residents of Dhobiatalla. Participants were identified through purposive sampling geared toward maximum variation (Lincoln and Guba, 1985) among borrowers and non-borrowers with regard to gender, age, religion, education, income, occupation, marital status, and family size. Participants were interviewed in Bengali or in Hindi, both individually and in focus groups in the slum. I used an interview guide that broadly focused on three main areas of interest: respondents' background characteristics, micro-enterprises, and strengths and constraints. I collected data in two phases. In the first phase, the interviews focused on the overall picture of residents: "Tell me about yourself, your family members, how you make a living. . . . " The second phase focused on identifying respondents' strengths and constraints. Data related to respondents' characteristics and how they made a living, which may have been tied to micro-enterprises, are reported here. I did not provide any financial incentive and informed respondents that their participation would not affect getting services from IMSE. Additionally, I interviewed the Director, staff, and board members of IMSE to get varying perspectives.

To guarantee methodological rigor, I first shared the preliminary findings with the Director of IMSE in early August 1995. Later, I shared these findings with respondents and IMSE's staff at a meeting held in the slum. The Director and staff of IMSE as well as the participants corroborated the findings. These two separate meetings served the research purpose of peer debriefing and member checks (Lincoln and Guba, 1985). Additionally, the meeting in the slum served an empowering function when respondents found out what was known about them. After returning to the United States, I analyzed quantifiable data through a SPSS/PC+ program and examined qualitative data, without the aid of qualitative software, for themes and variations among themes. Later, I shared qualitative data and themes with a colleague who teaches qualitative research for peer debriefing and for ascertaining validity of data interpretation. This colleague reaffirmed my findings.

Slum Background and Participants' Characteristics. Dhobiatalla slum is located close to a major commuting artery in east-central Calcutta. Its origin is tied to the 1964 Hindu-Muslim riots, when the Indian government rehabilitated 35 Muslim families there. In December 1992, another major Hindu-Muslim riot occurred in Calcutta, and Dhobiatalla was gutted in sporadic rioting that continued for four days. All residents fled their homes and took refuge in an emergency shelter. They lost everything. Residents had to start life afresh after returning to Dhobiatalla. They rebuilt their homes from scratch, restarted prior businesses, or looked for new work. Emergency cash and in-kind relief poured in from private and public sectors. Relief, however, is always temporary. IMSE, believing that self-efficacy is preferable to short-term aid, decided to extend micro-credit so that residents could start, or continue their own micro-enterprises.

Prior to starting its credit management program, IMSE surveyed Dhobiatalla in early 1993 and found that 1,006 families lived in a two-and-one-half acre area. Assuming average family size to be six, IMSE estimated that 6,000 people lived in Dhobiatalla. Most residents were Muslims, a minority population in India. In 1993, IMSE received funds from Action Aid, a London-based donor agency, and Rajiv Gandhi Foundation in India to start an urban micro-enterprise development program. IMSE spent 125,000 Rupees (Indian Currency, abbreviated as Rs) (US\$3,906) on loans ranging from Rs 300 (US\$9) to Rs 10,000 (US\$313) for 149 slum-dwellers. Of the 40 residents interviewed in this study, 17 (42.5%) took out loans from IMSE, whereas 23 (57.5%) did not. Table 1 shows the characteristics of participants.

The Grameen Model of Credit Management. I determined how and why the Grameen model of credit management works in Dhobiatalla through discussions with IMSE's Director, staff, participants, and by attending two center meetings. IMSE adapted the Grameen model of lending to suit local conditions. IMSE extended credit to both men and women to start micro-enterprises. IMSE's staff, in collaboration with the slum's Masjid Committee, first created a list of eligible borrowers based on income and employability. Like Grameen, IMSE did not train borrowers to start a business, nor did it require collateral. Instead, like Grameen, it created groups and centers or processes that were crucial for the functioning of the model.

At its smallest level, through the initiative of IMSE's social worker, five individuals who knew one another and had common interests but were not related by blood formed a group; six groups of five members each formed a center. The main assumptions behind forming groups and centers were: (a) individuals living in a community would know one another personally; (b) knowing one another would help them decide who to trust and who to work with on a long-term basis; and (c) personal relationships would provide support as well as create pressure to invest the loan wisely and return the funds in a timely manner. Group membership was crucial because if a member defaulted, no other members of the group could get a loan. Thus, the group served as the guarantor for the loan repayment.

It took a few weeks for five groups and a center to form. First, interested individuals had to participate in "continuous training," which involved learning rules and regulations related to loans, and the "Sixteen Decisions," a set of rules that helped focus individuals' efforts on improv-

TABLE 1. Participants' Characteristics (n = 40)

	The Borrower Micro-Entrepreneurs (n = 17)		The Non-Borrowers (n = 23)	
	Number	Percent	Number	Percent
Gender				
Female	10	59	13	57
Male	7	41	10	43
Age Range	25 to 65 years; mean = 40, sd = 11		22 to 60 years; mean = 41, sd = 13	
Religion				
Hindu	2	12	1	4
Muslim	15	88	22	96
Marital Status				
Married	13	76	16	70
Divorced	2	12	0	0
Widowed	2	12	6	26
Single	0	0	1	4
Education				
Illiterate	11	65	17	74
Literate	6	35	6	26
Income Range	Rs 500-5,000 (US$16.-$156.)/mth		Rs 100-7,000 (US$3.-$219.)/mth	
	mean=Rs 2,071 (US$65); sd = Rs 1,330 (US$42)		mean=Rs 1,373 (US$43.); sd = Rs 1,473 (US$46.)	
Occupation				
Self-employed	17	100	11	48
Work for Other	0	0	11	48
Unemployed	0	0	1	6
Extended Family				
Living in Slum	9	53	8	35
Living Elsewhere	5	29	7	30
None	3	18	8	35
Origin				
Bihar	5	29	13	57
Uttar Pradesh	3	18	6	26
Bengal	9	53	2	9
Bangladesh	0	0	2	9
Length of Stay	Ranges from 9 yrs to 31 yrs		Ranges from 7 yrs to 30 yrs	
	mean = 23 yrs; sd = 7 yrs		mean = 18 yrs; sd = 7 yrs	

ing their family lives and communities, such as keeping families small and helping one another (see Counts, 1996; Holcombe, 1995 for details). After interested individuals demonstrated their knowledge of the loan operation and participated in weekly center meetings, they were formally recognized by IMSE's staff and other borrowers as group members. Additionally, during this initial period, each individual developed a business plan that had to be approved by all members of the group before IMSE could accept it for loan processing. Once approved by IMSE's staff, two of a group's five members who were at the most advanced stage of starting a business received loans. If these two members repaid the loan regularly for two months, two more members of the same group became eligible for loans. If all four members consistently made payments for another two months, the fifth member got a loan.

In practice, when a member could not repay a loan, other members of the group and sometimes the center, worked out a solution that assured repayment. IMSE's staff were not always involved in this problem-solving process. A group leader said, "I persuaded some members to repay the loan on time. . . . Once when it was clear that Sabina could not repay the loan, we as a group paid in extra money on her behalf. Later she repaid us." IMSE charged a 10% interest or service fee for the loan and borrowers had to save weekly by putting in 1% of the loan in a Group Fund, and another 1% in an Emergency Fund. The money in the Group Fund initially belonged to the group and, over the year, could be used for emergencies such as inability to pay a loan installment. At the end of the year, fully paying borrowers got the money back as their personal savings. The Emergency Fund belonged to the entire center and at the end of the year, the members would decide how to use it. Further, weekly instead of annual repayment facilitated a low default rate.

IMSE's staff met weekly with the center in the slum. In a complete center meeting, six rows of five groups made weekly repayments, made deposits to savings accounts, and discussed new loan requests or other matters of interest to members. All business, especially exchange of money and discussion of loans, was carried out openly so that everyone knew what was going on. This reduced the opportunity for corruption and increased the chances for members to take responsibility.

Each group elected a chair and a secretary; the center elected a chief and a deputy chief. Each group's and center's elected officers served for one year and could not be re-elected until all others eligible had the opportunity to serve in a leadership position. Election and rotation of officers, and regular attendance and participation by all members under-scored the importance of the social empowerment and community development aspects of the Grameen model. Over time, participation either as a member or as an elected official of a group or the center offered members opportunities for acquiring self-confidence, leadership skills, and awareness to take on other actions.

An IMSE staff member explained, "over and above the businesses and the loans, we discuss matters related to health, education, nutrition, environment, public health, and family problems." In the Grameen model, awareness building, consciousness-raising, and leadership development followed rather than preceded delivery of credit services. The Director of IMSE said, "When people are hungry, they don't care about consciousness-raising activities. The credit enables people to start a business and feed themselves. Once they have basic food, clothes, and shelter, then it makes sense to talk about other issues with them. In rural areas, where we have been working longer . . . individuals have developed skills to undertake self-help activities. Now they demand entitlements from government departments."

In short, it became clear that group structure and processes were key to the economic and the socio-political successes of the Grameen model. Minor fine-tuning allowed the rural-oriented model to work in an urban setting of a different country. Additionally, it appeared that a successful micro-enterprise program required: (a) regular and consistent presence of a social worker who believed in people's strengths, reached out to people creatively, and knew and was trusted by the community; (b) a credit manager who attended to the financial details of loans; and (c) agency fund availability. Last but most importantly, the agency executive director played a critical role in program success through a strong belief in people, and micro-enterprise development as an anti-poverty strategy.

The Borrower Micro-Entrepreneurs. Among the 40 residents interviewed, 28 (70%) were micro-entrepreneurs. Seventeen of these 28 residents had obtained loans from IMSE. Thus, to avoid confusion, participants have been classified as borrower micro-entrepreneurs and non-borrowers. Of the 17 borrower micro-entrepreneurs, 10 (59%) were female and seven (41%) were male. Their ages ranged from 25 to 65 years; the average age was 40 years. Most were Muslims, two were Hindus. Their monthly income ranged from a low of Rs 500 (US$16) to a high of Rs 5,000 (US$156); average income per month was Rs 2,071 (US $65). The amount of loans varied from Rs 300 (US$9) to Rs 5,500 (S$172) and the average loan amount was Rs 1,747 (US $55).

The borrowers had three types of micro-enterprises: recycling, selling groceries, and "other." By and large, these micro-entrepreneurs created business opportunities that favored their skills, abilities, experiences, risk propensity, and capacity for capital outlay. Eight respondents operated recycling businesses such as cleaning used ball-point pen refills; sorting used paper, bottles, plastic, and coal; beating used batteries to remove and reuse aluminum and copper; and buying used furniture to resell. Further, some micro-enterprises were specifically geared towards meeting the local slum's needs. Thus, four participants sold groceries in or outside the slum; one man sold snacks, "paan," and cigarettes in one part of the slum, while another woman sold tea and snacks diametrically opposite his business. Rakella Bibi, a young mother of two, sold spices, essential in Indian cooking, in the slum. Luna Mondol, an elderly Hindu widow, sold fish in a market place just outside the slum.

Five participants had unique businesses that were categorized as "other." Two participants bought raw leather cheaply from the neighboring abattoir, treated the raw leather, and then sold the treated leather, which was used for making handbags and briefcases by others. Meena Bibi, a middle-aged Muslim divorced mother of six, and group leader, sold men's and women's clothes on installment plans in the slum. Raka Mondol had a part-time job as a nurse's aid, but took out a loan so that her husband could continue with their book-binding business outside the slum. Shamim, a young married Muslim man, started an electrical shop serving the slum and adjacent communities.

All borrower micro-entrepreneurs started their businesses immediately after taking out loans because the first installment of the loan was due within the first week of loan disbursement. All businesses except two were sole proprietorships. Five participants started new businesses and 12 continued with previous businesses. Four businesses required earlier skills training and the rest were semi-skilled or unskilled operations.

Micro-Enterprise Outcomes. A credit management program operating for less than two years is too young to manifest all socio-economic-political ramifications. Nevertheless, I saw some economic and psycho-social gains. From an economic point of view, there was a significant difference in income between borrower micro-entrepreneurs and non-borrowers when the income of the richest resident (Rs 7,000 or US$219) was dropped from analysis; he was ineligible for a loan due to high income. T-tests showed no significant differences (alpha = .05) in any demographic characteristic between borrowers and non-borrowers except income (t = 2.59, p = .02). All borrowers echoed the sentiment: "After I lost everything in the riot, the loan helped a great deal. It served as seed money for restarting my life. At least I could feed my family." They considered the 10% interest charged by IMSE as a service fee minuscule, compared to the market interest rate of 200% charged by money lenders.

All borrowers said that income from the micro-enterprise was enough to allow them to live well by their own standards. Seven borrowers rented and ten owned their homes; the owners had their own homes prior to participating in IMSE's micro-enterprise program. But, income from micro-enterprises enabled some to purchase furniture, television sets, and jewelry. Four participants involved family members in their business, while five employed outsiders. Not many saved money after paying for basic needs and repaying the loan, but a few saved and reinvested the capital into their existing business. All participants who had repaid their loans in full were eligible for new loans, and all of them, feeling more confident, had applied for and obtained much larger loans. Armina Bibi, a young, illiterate, divorced mother of three, and one of the poorest participants, cleaned used ball-point pen refills; she took out a loan of Rs 2,000 (US$63) the second year; her first loan was for Rs 700 (US$22).

In July 1995, 71% or 12 of the 17 borrowers had repaid their loans fully, four had partially repaid their loans, and one had not returned any money; all except one were still operating their businesses. There was no gender difference in loan repayment pattern: six males and six females had repaid their loans fully, one man and three women had partially repaid their loans, and a female borrower had not repaid any money because of business loss. She lost her entire loan because her investor was murdered and there was no mechanism to get the money back. She repaid IMSE through free labor such as cleaning the IMSE office and representing IMSE to outsiders. Those who had not repaid their loans fully cited various reasons for non-repayment such ill-health and unforeseen circumstances. A common reason for non-repayment was fear that IMSE would leave Dhobiatalla once all loans were repaid. Also, local money lenders who charged 200% interest on loans were unhappy with IMSE's credit extension at a 10% interest rate. They started a rumor that it was not necessary to repay the loan because IMSE had obtained funding, after the riot, to be given as a grant. When IMSE started disbursing loans for the second time at Dhobiatalla in July 1995 to fully paying members, many partially paid borrowers started repaying their dues because they, too, wanted new and larger loans.

The Non-Borrowers. Table 1 shows that the demographics of those who did not take out loans were very similar to the borrower micro-entrepreneurs. Further, 11 (48%) of 23 non-borrowers were self-employed micro-entrepreneurs. Thus, the question is, "What held this group back from taking out loans?" One man had a high income and was ineligible for a loan; another woman had a financially resourceful extended family and did not need an external loan. However, there were nine micro-entrepreneurs or self-employed participants who were eligible for loans, but did not access them. Most sold seasonal fruit both inside and outside the slum. Listening to the stories of the remaining 21 participants (including the nine self-employed), it became clear that some would have benefited from loans but did not take them out for various psycho-social reasons.

The main hurdles against taking out a loan or starting a micro-enterprise were: lack of familiarity with a loan program; lack of knowledge about IMSE's loan program; distrust of a new agency; fear of being unable to repay the loan; lack of social support leading to lower level of courage to start a new venture; lack of experience with micro-enterprise development in an urban area (shorter length of stay at Dhobiatalla); gender role expectations imposed on younger married women; lack of child care; and lack of security with an unknown business venture, as opposed to a low-paying job. However, after observing the successes of the first batch of borrowers, some of these cautious analyzers became more open to obtaining a loan and had taken the necessary steps for loan application.

Examining the themes of stories of all 40 participants, I observed that high-income generating micro-enterprises were tied to: (a) immigration from another state to Calcutta, (b) longer stay at Dhobiatalla, and (c) extended family living in Dhobiatalla. Stories revealed that most early immigrants struggled initially and engaged in small trade. Slowly, they built their businesses as they became more familiar with the environmental resources. Later, when business opportunities and resources were discovered, they shared this privileged information with kinship groups rather than publicly. Prior entrepreneurial success encouraged most to take out a loan from IMSE, and business successes of extended family living in the slum kindled hope and courage among younger members to take risks with micro-enterprises as well as to take out a loan from IMSE. Observing the successes of early micro-entrepreneurs, some residents who immigrated later and did not have kinship support living in Dhobiatalla also decided to take risks and started their own small businesses. Overall, micro-enterprises created a culture that had rippling effects on family members, kinship groups, non-borrowers, and the community.

DISCUSSION AND IMPLICATIONS

The findings of this study are similar to other studies (Counts, 1996; Else and Raheim, 1992; Holcombe, 1995; Raheim, 1996; Solomon, 1992), which suggests the feasibility of micro-enterprise development projects as an anti-poverty strategy and an empowerment tool for people living in impoverished communities. The most important implications of this study are: (a) micro-lending for micro-enterprise development has a significant economic impact on participants; and (b) micro-enterprise development creates a culture that has rippling effects on a community. These findings are important because they indicate that micro-enterprises create economic self-sufficiency and encourage others to emulate such ventures leading to a micro-entrepreneurial culture within a community.

Considering the historic context in which IMSE started its micro-lending program in Dhobiatalla, that is, the riot that completely dismantled the slum, it is noteworthy that the study found significantly higher incomes in borrower micro-entrepreneurs compared to non-borrowers within two years. Although micro-lending was crucial, it was not the only factor that contributed to significant increases in income. Prior entrepreneurial experience played a major role in taking out loans and continuing businesses. However, micro-lending for micro-enterprises had socio-economic ramifications for individuals as well as for the community. Ability to repay a small loan built confidence among borrowers who re-applied for much larger loans and defaulters began repaying in the hope of obtaining a larger loan. Micro-enterprises created a fund base in the community and provided employment for some local residents. Funds remained in the community as residents used complimentary services provided by one another through their micro-enterprises. Moreover, economic gains of borrowers served a role modeling function for others who later became more open to taking out loans. Thus, micro-lending for micro-enterprises not only generated income but also had many kinds and levels of rippling effects on an impoverished community.

Major socio-economic-political implications of micro-enterprise development, noted in other studies, such as better health, education, family stability, home ownership, and self-esteem were not highly evident in this study. It is possible that this is due to the short duration of the micro-lending program. It was especially disturbing to note the high illiteracy rate among participants (not a single resident of Dhobiatalla was a high school graduate), and their lack of concern with their children's education. Some respondents, both borrowers and non-borrowers, sent their children to school; however, there was no strong pattern of school attendance among borrowers' children. Long-standing high unemployment rates among educated youth in Calcutta were the primary reason for a lack of concern with children's education. However, both borrowers and non-borrowers stressed the value of skills training for their children. Many non-borrowers' children worked as apprentices. The borrowers tended to engage their children in family micro-enterprises, another reflection of how an entrepreneurial culture is created and continued and a major reflection of the socio-economic realities of living in an impoverished community.

On the positive side, home visits and observations indicated that housing, health, nutrition, as well as clothing and other material possessions, all of which have some association with income, were better among some borrowers than non-borrowers. I did not observe a significant pattern of well-being among borrowers in relation to non-borrowers. However, both groups displayed hope, aspiration, and capacities for moving forward almost universally. A longitudinal study is required to demonstrate the full range of effects of a micro-enterprise development program in Dhobiatalla.

Because micro-enterprises had rippling effects on individuals as well as on a community, this study has important lessons for social workers promoting micro-enterprise development projects in poor U.S. communities. There is a wide-spread belief in the United States, however, that micro-enterprises work only in developing countries where there is dire poverty. If the existence of dire poverty alone makes micro-enterprises work in developing countries, then micro-enterprises should work also in developed countries because poverty in developed and developing countries is more similar than dissimilar (Counts, 1996; Lusk and Stoesz, 1994; Sen, 1995). But it is the differences between developed and developing nations that account for some of the successes of micro-enterprises in developing countries. A few such differences are: unregulated market conditions that thrive on low-skilled enterprises; absence of income maintenance programs; availability of free health care; and a lower cost of living. A person like Armina Bibi, who somehow survived in Calcutta by cleaning and selling used ball-point pen refills, could not survive in the United States because: (a) ball-point pen refills are not recycled here; and (b) her income would be inadequate to pay for rent and health care after buying food and clothes for her family. However, the crucial point in Armina's story is that a micro-loan allowed Armina to make a new beginning–to start a micro-enterprise, to take care of her family, and to eventually expand her business. Similarly, a micro-loan would enable some in the United States to make new beginnings.

In the United States, the nature of micro-enterprises, the terms and conditions of loans, as well as the amounts of loans are likely to be different from those in developing nations. Nonetheless, a micro-credit is the key that holds the promise of opening doors to earning a living and eventually revitalizing poor communities. Opportunities for starting micro-enterprises that meet local needs are as prevalent here as they are in developing nations. Despite its many harsh implications, the Welfare Reform Act of 1996 has created many opportunities for low-income individuals to start micro-enterprises. For example, those who are forced to join the labor force as a result of the welfare reform will require many services, such as child care, transportation, affordable clothing, and beauty care to go to work, all of which could be provided by micro-entrepreneurs.

Given this scenario, social workers could combine micro-meso and macro level strategies with micro-enterprise development to bring about changes in marginalized communities. Thus, social workers could work with their state governments to remove policy barriers that impede micro-enterprise development, and utilize available block grant funds to create micro-enterprise development programs for people living in impoverished communities. Such a program could adapt the Grameen model of peer lending and encourage five members to provide complimentary services needed by neighbors joining the labor force. Within this framework, those who prefer self-employment to wage employment could gain economic self-sufficiency by providing much needed services to neighbors. This way, funds would remain within the community as neighbors would seek and purchase services from one another rather than from outside agencies. Because of a lack of micro-entrepreneurial history in poor communities, initially, not many residents may join the program. But, it is likely that with time, many others would start their own micro-enterprises after they observe the successes of the early micro-entrepreneurs. Slowly, a culture of micro-entrepreneurship would take root in U.S. communities, which could potentially change the current blighted face of disintegrating and impoverished communities.

Additionally, the study suggests that social workers have a role to play in micro-enterprise program implementation. Social workers need to work with participants to find out what aspects of the program design promote or impede micro-enterprise development. For example, the study found that some borrowers thought IMSE's program so helpful that they decided not to repay their loans on time, thinking this might make IMSE continue its program at Dhobiatalla. Once this finding was shared with IMSE's staff and IMSE started the second round of loan disbursals, many started repaying their loans in order to get larger loans. Certainly, this was idiosyncratic behavior that any program design would not have anticipated. Thus, it appears that by working with participants daily, it is possible for social workers to find out what is working well and what is not working well with the program. This knowledge would then be used to clarify program components to make micro-enterprise programs work for participants. In the United States, it is unlikely that borrowers default on loans intentionally because of the existing credit reporting system. However, social workers may find out that the level of business training offered to prospective borrowers is not appropriate for them, leading to fewer micro-enterprise start-ups.

So far, micro-enterprise development projects have not had a very strong impact in the United States because there are so few of them and they are so new. It is possible that a micro-entrepreneurial culture with the rippling effects observed in Calcutta will also become evident when many low-income individuals start their own micro-enterprises here. Many more social workers need to learn more about micro-enterprises and their ramifications. We need to believe in our clients' strengths as well as in our own strengths. Together, we can promote, sustain, and invigorate a micro-enterprise development movement across the United States. Empowered with economic self-sufficiency afforded through micro-enterprises, many of our clients living in impoverished communities could unshackle the chains of poverty around them and, over time, create their desired communities.

REFERENCES

Ashe, J. (1985). *The PISCES II Experience: Local efforts in micro-enterprise development*. Washington, DC: Agency for International development.

Balkin, S. (1989). *Self-employment for low-income people*. New York: Praeger.

Bandyopadhyay, D. (1989). Poverty alleviation through special employment programmes in rural India. In M. Muqtada (Ed.) *The elusive target: An evaluation of target-group approaches to employment creation in rural Asia* (pp. 79-135). Geneva, Switzerland: Asian Regional Team for Employment Promotion, International Labour Organization.

Bandyopadhyay, D. (1985). An evaluation of policies and programmes for the alleviation of rural poverty in India. In Rizwanul Islam (Ed.) *Strategies for alleviating poverty in rural Asia* (pp. 99-151). Dhaka: Bangladesh Institute of Development Studies.

Baydas, M.M., Meyer, R.L., & Aguilera-Alfred, N. (1994). Credit rationing in small-scale enterprises: Special microenterprise programs in Ecuador. *Journal of Development Studies, 31*(2), 279-288.

Bornstein, D. (1996). *The price of a dream: The story of the Grameen Bank and the idea that is helping the poor to change their lives*. New York: Simon & Schuster.

Clark, M., Huston, T., & Meister, B. (Eds.) (1997). *1996 directory of U.S. microenterprise programs*. Washington DC: The Self-Employment Learning Project, The Aspen Institute.

Counts, A. (1996). *Give us credit*. New York: Random House.

de Soto, H. (1989). *The other path: The invisible revolution in the third world*. New York: Harper & Row.

Dutta, B. (1996). India: Tradition for poverty research. In Oyen, E., Miller, S. M., & Samad, S. A. (Eds.) *Poverty: A global review* (pp. 100-122). Oslo: Scandinavian University Press.

Edgcomb, E., Klein, J., & Clark, P. (1996). *The practice of microenterprise in the U.S.* Washington, DC: The Self-Employment Learning Project, The Aspen Institute.

Else, J.F., & Raheim, S. (1992). AFDC clients as entrepreneurs: Self-employment offers an important option. *Public Welfare, 50*(4), 36-41.

Evans, C. (1996). *Poverty alleviation through micro-enterprise development.* Luncheon Address at the Second Golden Door Knob Meeting of the First Step Fund, March 29, Kansas City, Missouri.

Holcombe, S. (1995). *Managing to empower: The Grameen Bank's experience of poverty alleviation.* London: Zed Books.

Holloway, M., & Wallich, P. (1992). A risk worth taking. *Scientific American, 267*(5), 126.

Hossain, M. (1988). *Credit for alleviation of rural poverty: The Grameen Bank in Bangladesh.* International Food Research Institute in collaboration with the Bangladesh Institute of Development Studies Research Report 65. International Food Policy Research Institute.

Institute for Financial Management and Research. (1984). *An economic assessment of poverty eradication and rural unemployment alleviation programme and their prospects.* Madras: Institute for Financial Management and Research.

Jain, P.S. (1996). Managing credit for the rural poor: Lessons from the Grameen Bank. *World Development, 24*(1), 79-89.

Johnson, K. (1994). Making a big deal out of nothing. *State Legislatures, 20*(6), 24-27.

Kamaluddin, S. (1993). Lender with a mission: Bangladesh's Grameen Bank targets poorest of poor. *Far Eastern Economic Review, 156*(11), 38-40.

Klein, J. (1995). Mothers vs. Mullahs: A program favored by Hillary Clinton meets Islamic resistance. *Newsweek, 125*(16), 56.

Lincoln, Y.S., & Guba, E.G. (1985). *Naturalistic inquiry.* Newbury Park, CA: Sage Publications.

Lusk, M.W., & Stoesz, D. (1994). International social work in a global economy. *Journal of Multicultural Social Work, 3*(2), 101-113.

Margolis, J. (1996). When a little money goes a long way. *Canadian Banker, 103*(1), 26-28.

Morewagae, B.S., Rempel, H., & Seemule, M. (1995). Access to credit for non-formal micro-enterprises in Botswana. *Journal of Development Studies, 31*(3), 481-504.

National Bank for Agriculture and Rural Development. (1984). *Study of implementation of Integrated Rural Development Programme.* Bombay: National Bank for Agriculture and Rural Development.

Programme Evaluation Organization. (1985). *Evaluation report on Integrated Rural Development Programme.* New Delhi: Planning Commission, Government of India, Programme Evaluation Organization.

Puls, B. (1988). *From unemployed to self-employed: A program analysis.* Washington, DC: National Conference of State Legislators.

Raheim, S. (1997). Problems and prospects of self-employment as an economic independence option for welfare recipients. *Social Work, 42*(1), 44-53.

Raheim, S. (1996). Micro-enterprise as an approach for promoting economic development in social work: lessons from the Self-Employment Investment Demonstration. *International Social Work, 39,* 69-82.

Rahman, A., & Wahid, A.N.M. (1992). The Grameen Bank and the changing patron-client relationship in Bangladesh. *Journal of Contemporary Asia, 22*(3), 303-321.

Reserve Bank of India. (1984). *Implementation of Integrated Rural Development Programme: A field study.* Rural Planning and Credit Department, Central Office, Bombay: Reserve Bank of India.

Rose, K. (1992). *Where women are leaders: The SEWA movement in India.* London: Zed Books.

Sen, A. (1995, September). *Social development: National and international.* Benjamin Youngdahl Lecture Series, Washington University-St. Louis.

Solomon, L.D. (1992). Microenterprise: Human reconstruction in America's inner cities. *Harvard Journal of Law & Public Policy, 5*(1), 191-221.

Spalter-Roth, R.M., Soto, E., & Zandniapour, L. (1994). *Micro-enterprise and women: The viability of self employment as a strategy for alleviating poverty.* Washington, DC: Institute for Women's Policy Research.

Spodek, H. (1994). The self-employed women's association (SEWA) in India: Feminist, Gandhian power in development. *Economic Development and Cultural Change, 43*(1), 193-202.

Tameen, M.S. (1990). Foreign aid–treating the symptoms: Misunderstanding the microenterprise. *Reason, 22*(June 1990), 40-41.

Tyler, P. (1995). Star at conference on women: Banker who lends to the poor. *The New York Times,* September 14, A6.

Weil, M.O., and Gamble, D.N. (1995). Community practice models. In *Encyclopedia of Social Work,* pp. 577-594, 19th Edition, Washington, DC: NASW Press.

WIN News. (1995). India: The success of SEWA: Self-Employed Women's Association. *WIN News, 21* (3), 62.

Yunus, M. (1995). Grameen Bank: Experiences and reflections. *Impact, 30*(3-4), 13-25.

Yunus, M. (1990). Credit and ingenuity can save the children. *The Los Angeles Times,* July 9 at B5.

Yunus, M. (1987). The poor as the engine of development. *The Washington Quarterly, 10*(4), 139-145.

Southeastern Women's Involvement in Sustainable Development Efforts: Their Roles and Concerns

Evonne Lack, MSW
Dorothy N. Gamble, MSW

SUMMARY. Sustainable development takes into account the social and economic needs of people in communities, as well as the urgent concerns for environmental protection. Women's roles in sustainable development are of particular interest in light of the numerous environmentally related grassroots development initiatives taken by women throughout the world. In preparation for a participatory forum addressing women's roles in sustainable development, we conducted a survey among representatives from Southeastern grassroots organizations working on community development projects. The results indicate a sustainable development focus in grassroots women's development efforts, as well as a need for networking, skills training, and opportunities to share project experience. *[Article copies available for a fee from The Haworth Document Delivery Service: 1-800-342-9678. E-mail address: getinfo@haworthpressinc.com]*

Evonne Lack completed her MSW at the University of North Carolina at Chapel Hill and was a research assistant for the Women, Community and Sustainable Development Project.

Dorothy N. Gamble is a Clinical Assistant Professor, Assistant Dean for Student Services, and Co-Project Director for the Women, Community and Sustainable Development Project at the School of Social Work, University of North Carolina at Chapel Hill.

[Haworth co-indexing entry note]: "Southeastern Women's Involvement in Sustainable Development Efforts: Their Roles and Concerns." Lack, Evonne, and Dorothy N. Gamble. Co-published simultaneously in *Journal of Community Practice* (The Haworth Press, Inc.) Vol. 5, No. 1/2, 1998, pp. 85-101; and: *Community Economic Development and Social Work* (ed: Margaret S. Sherraden, and William A. Ninacs) The Haworth Press, Inc., 1998, pp. 85-101. Single or multiple copies of this article are available for a fee from The Haworth Document Delivery Service [1-800-342-9678, 9:00 a.m. - 5:00 p.m. (EST). E-mail address: getinfo@haworthpressinc.com].

85

It is useful to consider community economic development within the larger concept of sustainable development. In recent years, we have seen a variety of new perspectives on development models, and significant challenges to older models for their failure to diminish poverty and curb destruction of the earth's natural resources. Sustainable development provides a new paradigm for linking community social and economic development to a more holistic, overarching model that also includes care of the earth (Estes, 1993).

Sustainable development draws on historical, even ancient ideas that link human and natural spheres as parts of a whole. The report of the World Commission on Environment and Development (1987), headed by Gro Harlem Brundtland, reconceptualizes sustainable development to consider the social and economic needs of people in communities, as well as the urgent concerns for global environmental protection. Among the goals of sustainable development that the report describes are the "judicious use of the planet's nonrenewable physical resources, and a balance between economic, social, cultural, and physical development" (1993, p. 13).

It is also important to clarify the link between social work and sustainable development. Social work's person-in-environment perspective provides the framework for the profession to be engaged in sustainable development efforts. Hoff and McNutt (1994) have challenged social work to stretch the person-in-environment model to include concern for the natural world, often neglected in the social system assessment and intervention efforts in which social workers engage. The concept of sustainable development connects our work at the grassroots level with holistic methods that call for a balance among the economic, social, cultural, and physical aspects of development. The principles of sustainable development that speak to intergenerational care for the environment and social justice concerns related to access of resources and location of waste disposal connect easily, in our view, with social work empowerment practice. When we can think of the people and communities with whom we work as part of a whole organic universe, our tasks are shaped by partnerships, by participation, by gender and cultural sensitivity, by caring, and by learning.

WOMEN IN SUSTAINABLE DEVELOPMENT

When development is viewed solely in terms of economic growth, we think in terms of the dominant development model, which focuses on the efficiency of a free market for allocation of resources and production opportunities. This dominant model has been challenged for its wanton destruction of the environment (Berry, 1989), its frequent disregard of human and cultural needs (Daly and Cobb, 1989; Korten, 1995), and its contribution to the powerlessness of women and people of color (Harcourt, 1994). Women, according to Harcourt (1994), argue that gender bias in the dominant development model prevents gender equity and ignores women's contributions to the economy as well as their role in the management of the environment. Furthermore, " . . . development theory and practice founded on Western biases and assumptions excludes both women and nature from its understanding of development and, in so doing, has contributed to the current economic and ecological crisis" (p. 3).

Sustainable development, as it is emerging, gives human services professionals the opportunity to think in ecological terms, to think of ourselves and those with whom we work, not as separate struggling individuals, but as part of a whole living earth. In the sustainable development model, solutions emerge through participatory efforts that pay particular attention to the roles of gender, culture, family, and community in finding ways to a healthier future. Analysis of social problems encompasses a larger contextual model including the physical, historical, cultural, political, and economic aspects of human existence. This kind of analysis could enable us to see the more spiritual connection between human societies and the earth, as described by Berry (1989). Sustainable development helps us connect with a message that people in Appalachia know so well: a threat to the environment is a threat to ourselves, our families, our communities, and our future. In the words of Maxine Waller, "In years past, we've relied on the land to take care of us, and it did. And I think it's high time that we started taking care of the land" (Hinsdale, Lewis and Waller, 1995, p. 98).

Linking Sustainable Development in the World and in the Southeastern United States

Some observers have condemned structural adjustment policies imposed on the developing world to moderate the debt burden of countries with loans from the World Bank and International Monetary Fund, saying that they exert a special burden on women and children whose economic conditions have worsened during the late 1980s (Renshaw, 1995). In a sense, a different kind of structural adjustment has been taking place in the southeastern United States due to the gradual structural removal of the traditional modes of economic security, both agricultural and industrial. Many traditional industrial anchors of southern communities, mining and textiles as examples, have simply disappeared, divesting communities of the source of economic income they had counted upon for generations. In agriculture, small land holdings in tobacco had provided a comfortable economic existence for many rural families over generations. As tobacco companies were able to secure a cheaper source of leaf in foreign markets, and the concern for the health costs of tobacco use in this country grew, small farms were often lost to larger agri-businesses engaged in hog and poultry production. While not as defined as the World Bank's stated policies for structural adjustment, these changes indicate a decided "structural adjustment" in the southeastern United States of a more gradual nature, completely changing the opportunities for economic security. In addition to the economic decline of many areas of the Southeast, communities have begun to examine and challenge industrial and agricultural policies that left their environment degraded and uninhabitable (Hall, 1988).

Women's Roles in Development

There are so many stories from around the world of the particular roles women play in building community organizations for the purpose of reviving community as a place for families not just to survive, but to develop (Creevey, 1996; Young, 1993). *SEEDS 2* (Leonard, 1995) describes examples from Zambia, Mozambique, Sudan, Thailand, India, and North America. These examples analyze the "practical everyday basic needs" of women as well as "more strategic long-term needs." In their case study of Ivanhoe, West Virginia, Hinsdale, Lewis and Waller (1995) describe the strength, new structural forms, and people-centered focus of women-led community development organizations in Appalachia. Examining the role of women in development efforts is particularly important as women are increasingly influential in shaping the rebirth of communities worldwide.

From United Nations data we know that in developing regions of the world one in three households is totally dependent on a woman for its livelihood and 70% of small enterprises are run by women (UNIFEM, 1993). We also know that while women have made great strides in education, still two-thirds of the world's illiterates are women as a result of complex factors relating to variable gender expectations within families and discriminatory educational policies. Finally, we know that assisting women to gain education and skills in social and economic development will significantly improve the health and development of families and communities (United Nations Development Program, 1996). Our interest was in discovering how these trends worldwide were similar or different for women in the many economically depressed, "developing" communities of the South. We wanted to know if southern development efforts were related to the more holistic ideas of sustainable development, including gender and culture sensitivity, caring for the earth, and concern for nonrenewable resources. Further, we were interested in exploring, from the perspective of the participant, the skill and knowledge needs of people, especially women, engaged in development in rural southern communities.

RESEARCH METHODS

The Use of Qualitative Research to Analyze the Context of Development

To address these questions, we undertook a qualitative research project involving a telephone survey of grassroots workers throughout the southeastern United States. We focused on projects managed by women or specifically addressing women's issues.

We used qualitative methods in this inquiry to gain a more powerful, deeper understanding of the context of the issues from the perspectives of our respondents. According to Patton (1987), qualitative methods produce direct quotations that "reveal the respondents' levels of emotion, the way in which they have organized the world, their thoughts about what is happening, their experiences, and their basic perceptions" (p. 11). In addition to finding out what kinds of groups were doing women-focused sustainable development in the Southeast we wanted to know about the nature of the projects, their successes and failures, their general goals, and the skills and knowledge they needed to be more effective in reaching their goals. These broad areas of inquiry were a necessary beginning point of exploration because we had direct knowledge of only a few such projects in our home state. We did not know if the types of problems and issues people would identify would be similar or completely different. For longer-term purposes, we were curious to know if the problems and issues encountered by southeastern sustainable development projects were similar to those encountered by women in projects from India, Honduras, and Africa.

Our research interest was in determining the needs of these groups so that we could develop training activities and resource materials to help their grassroots leaders become more effective in community sustainable development projects. In the words of Marshall and Rossman (1995), we knew our efforts would require significant "recycling of concepts," until we had a sufficient exploratory and descriptive understanding of the issues facing the women in these projects. Our guiding principle was to collect information in the words of the respondents. The value of collecting indigenous knowledge about communities in the words of the community members has been clearly articulated by international scholars interested in development (Appleton, Fernandez, Hill, and Quiroz, 1996).

In future work, as we begin to relate directly with specific communities, our research approach will incorporate even more participatory methods. Community members will engage in determining what information will be most useful in making progress in their community development approaches and how they can gather and analyze that information. Such participatory methods are widely used today in the developing world and have been employed by the Highlander Center in Tennessee (Absalon, Mwayaya, and Johnson, 1996; Chambers, 1994; Gaventa, 1981; Noponen, 1996). Facilitating participatory research helps protect indigenous knowledge systems so that this knowledge is not lost, and so that community groups can incorporate "old" knowledge with new scientific and technological information, thereby customizing local development plans.

Snowball Sampling

We learned of several organizations through funders' recipient lists, as well as participant rosters from two sustainable development conferences. However, many of the smaller organizations would never have come to our attention if we had not used snowball sampling. At the conclusion of most interviews, we asked respondents if they knew of other projects similar to their own, and thus the study participants served as a major source for contacts. In researching issues affecting southeastern grassroots women, snowball sampling is vital to creating a representative sample population. This method enables the inclusion of smaller projects which may receive less funding and resources, and have few formal structures for publicizing their efforts.

Description of the Sample

Of the 59 contacts included in our sample, 58 participated in phone interviews and one responded by letter containing conference suggestions. The organizations represented are active in 11 different southern states, from Florida to Virginia. We included 50 women and nine men in the interviews. The sample represented a diverse group, ranging from legal assistance projects to citizen advocacy organizations and technical assistance projects. Eight organizations had a focus on sustainable agriculture, three focused on hazardous waste, nine were wide-ranging community development organizations, nine were micro-enterprise organizations, two concentrated on worker's rights and advocacy, three focused on eco-tourism, and four were single economic development enterprises. The remainder included service organizations, training programs, grant programs, and single and multi-issue political groups.

Description of Interviews

The interviews ranged in length from a few minutes to half an hour. The format was semi-structured. In most cases the interviewer began by briefly describing a planned forum on the topic of sustainable development, explaining to the respondent how our group had found out about the project, and asking the respondent if s/he would be willing to be interviewed. In 28 cases, participants were also asked what they would want to learn from a forum such as the one we were planning, and what other suggestions they had for us. Eleven participants were asked, as a follow-up question, to speculate on why there tended to be more women than men involved in their projects. In about 20 cases, the phone interview became an in-depth conversation that covered a wide range of topics. These included personal philosophies, frustrations, pride in past accomplishments, and hopes for the future of sustainable development work.

The semi-structured format enabled us to tailor the interview to the experiences and style of each participant. Some respondents were eager to describe their work and thoughts on women's involvement, and several thought out loud during the conversation, yielding data that was rich in honesty and depth. Others were initially reluctant to share their experiences and feelings, but opened up once the interviewer expressed genuine excitement about the work they described.

CENTRAL FINDINGS AND PRACTICE CONCERNS

Women's Roles and Ways of Knowing

Throughout the interview process, it became apparent that a large number of organizations did not overtly address women's issues, but were nevertheless managed largely by women. We asked several participants about their opinions on the reasons for women's overrepresentation, which led to many interesting discussions.

More than one participant noted women's public health concerns as an impetus for their involvement. For example, the director of a community development project focusing on hazardous waste suggested that the prevalence of women participants in her organization was indicative of their concern for public health issues (the organization began as a women's group with a strong public health focus). As she pointed out, women have reason to be alarmed; risk assessments for toxic emissions are based on measures for an average 160-pound male. The potential harm of these emissions is higher for women, small children, and babies in utero. She also speculated that, as a generality, "men are more likely to trust government" pollution control measures than women, while women are more apt to feel that the current standards are insufficient and thus are more likely to get involved in environmental work. An organizer from a comparable project expressed similar reasoning for his mostly female colleagues; he suggested that women get more involved with toxicity issues because of their interest in children's health. Similarly, the vice president of a public interest law firm with a strong emphasis on environmental issues said that most of the community members who get involved are women. She also attributed this involvement to women's focus on "the health of their children and families." She added that women "recognize on a gut level" that there is a problem, while men are more likely to "need scientific proof."

Others cited the unappealing nature of sustainable development in explaining women's overrepresentation. One participant said that women tend to be overrepresented in non-profits because the salaries are lower and "the work looks less attractive," a view corroborated by other participants. A similar perspective was expressed by a woman who said that men are more likely to be "too busy" with their careers to get involved in community work. As she stated, men may want community change but "women are the ones to come to the meetings."

Some participants pointed to more fundamental differences between women and men. One slant on this issue came from the former director of a far-reaching community change venture, where she said women were at the "heart" of the project. She suggested that men are "more predisposed to act in a businesslike way." They tend to see things in "red-black" extremes, while "women's roles today encompass so many things," including civic responsibilities, families, and personal interests. She stressed that people who work in community change efforts need "to be multi-visual." Another respondent estimated that 75% of the citizens participating in her community enterprise program were women. She said that this is because of women's "longer-term view" and their "greater capacity to go to the depths of seeing how things really are." She stated that particularly in Appalachia, environmental-economic development is "women's work," as women have "maintained a connection with the land and resources," and "can see the interrelatedness" of land and economy.

Another participant expressed the idea that women are better able to envision change; this woman's organization aids various community development projects. She explained that it is mostly women who approach her for help, whereas it is "difficult to enlist the men," because they have "difficulty being able to envision." In her opinion, men are more likely to experience feelings of "hopelessness," or to respond to community problems by violence. Women, on the other hand, are more likely to envision solutions and "work from the kitchen table."

The prevalence of women is not limited to the organizational structure; three of the four single economic development projects in our sample enlisted mainly women workers. For example, the initiator of a sewing factory that began as a community project said the factory had only one male employee. She attributed this to the lack of employment opportunities for women in the community.

Finally, the overrepresentation of women in sustainable development may be self-perpetuating. One participant said that because most of the staff in her organization were women, other women are more likely to become involved as staff or volunteers.

Evidently, women's opinions about their prevalence in sustainable development work are often reflective of their feelings regarding men's potential involvement. One woman emphasized the need for men to expand their roles in community change, because an "inordinate number of women head up nonprofits . . . but don't have a lot of resources." On the other hand, it is possible that some women may not trust that men can be involved without radically altering the focus. For example, one participant stated that when a grassroots group begins to "look important, the men show up and take it over." In her opinion, women need to be able to recognize this and, rather than stepping aside, stay with the project and work with the men. For agricultural women, she explained that "consciousness raising" is particularly difficult because they are often satisfied with doing half the work but none of the decision-making. Another participant noted that while women are at the forefront of grassroots organizations where the focus is on "basic needs," men "start to dominate" organizations that are more focused on economic development.

It seems that before men and women can collaborate effectively, these complicated gender dynamics need to be openly discussed. Workshops and other forums for discussion can heighten awareness of the potential problems resulting from working together. Women's concerns need to be heard, while men need to expand their focus to include sustainable development as both men's and women's work. In organizations where men are involved, women and men can communicate on an ongoing basis in order to avoid a reshuffling of roles in which men would dominate and women would merely assist.

Additionally, the overrepresentation of women need not be seen as negative. While men's participation will ultimately be important to the future of sustainable development, women may bring specific concerns and resources to their work that are vital to maintaining a sustainable development focus. One of the respondents quoted above, for example, said that many of the farms in her area have been lost because of overinvestment, which may not have happened "if women's and children's needs had been represented." Women can learn from each other's experiences, hardships, and triumphs; thus it is important that they collaborate. Male players who are already invested in sustainable development work may be particularly cognizant of this need. The director of a technical assistance project explained that her organization serves only women, and that she has had to turn men away from women-only trainings in the past. She said the men's reaction has not been negative, even when they have traveled from another area.

However, this attitude may be rare among men who are not already invested in sustainable development work. Thus it is not surprising that in some cases, it seems that women shy away from appearing as a "women's" group. Some organizations in our sample were careful not to appear to exclude men, despite women's extensive involvement. For example, the director of an organization that conducts sustainable development workshops for grassroots groups said that although many of the participants are women, they do not target workshops specifically for women because of the potential "divisive dynamics" that could result between spouses. This points to a larger issue of women's fear of being ostracized for appearing to be too affiliated with other women, or rejecting men. Fear of invoking stereotypes that come with women's groups may keep women from gathering together for support, or from collectively addressing concerns specific to them as women.

Lack of Access

The tension between grassroots women and the larger political, activist, and agricultural establishments came up in several conversations. For example, the director of a farm workers' organization noted that although the women who were involved were comfortable with leadership roles internally, they were not comfortable dealing with the state's "agricultural establishment," which is "very male." These outside organizations were often "not open to women leadership," and did not respect women farmers, despite the fact that many farms in the state are "family affairs" where women are heavily involved. In terms of local politics, another respondent stated that the "good old boy system is alive and well," and can include women as well as men. She emphasized the importance of recognizing this challenge and finding "alternate ways of working effectively toward change." Yet another participant pointed out the complications that can result from women organizers being related to community members. As she explained, this can "confuse women's roles." Women who are related to people in the community may have a difficult time breaking out of family roles and being respected in their work.

If women are barred from leadership roles, or if their leadership positions are not respected, they may be denied important resources. Lack of access to credit, for example, is particularly prohibitive. One participant, who founded and directs an agricultural training project, explained that women are often restricted from borrowing from the same source as their husbands, and thus are unable to develop their own businesses. Lack of day care is another barrier to women's involvement in educational or grassroots activities, noted by two participants who hope to expand their programs to include day care facilities.

In addition, family members may be resistant to changes in family structure resulting from women's participation in grassroots projects. One educator, who trains other women in sustainable farming, suggested including in future training a discussion of strategies to involve family members in "equalize[ing] the running of the household" so that women can "pursue their professions."

In terms of concrete resources, women may themselves internalize others' conceptions of their general unimportance, and thus struggle in a world made for men without discussing the need for practical information. One respondent who works with a grower's organization, for example, said that women farmers see the need to share information about "simple but essential" resources, such as smaller gloves and tools. However, they are often unwilling to discuss this at conferences because of the feeling that it is a negligible issue.

Finally, many participants emphasized their desire for practical information, such as funding strategies, grant writing, publicity, and managerial skills. It seems that networking and collaboration could enable women to not only share information, but also work together to identify ways to break down barriers and engender respect in their families and communities.

Rural and Urban Concerns

Two women noted conflicts between urban and rural agendas. The coordinator of a rural organization, for example, explained that people from rural areas who attend sustainable development conferences are often "dismayed by what urban people consider sustainable development," i.e., increased employment. She stated that this job creation can lead to the cheap removal of resources from rural areas, an issue to which urban players are not sensitive. She emphasized that the resulting "tension" between those living in urban and rural areas needs to be openly discussed. The director of an urban gardening employment project addressed another side of this issue, saying that she feels urban agendas are often marginalized at sustainable development conferences. She emphasized the need to include urban issues at training workshops, and suggested that "some of the best ideas could be practiced [in the Southeast] to keep these smaller size cities with just as big problems from being totally abandoned."

Differences between urban and rural conceptualizations of sustainable development are clearly an area for further research. It seems that in the Southeast, the lack of networking and communication between grassroots activists from urban and rural areas creates a serious barrier to important resources on both sides. For example, although rural areas may contain natural resources necessary for urban job creation, women in these areas lack technical support, which is more available in urban areas. Lack of technical support isolates rural women from each other, as exemplified by one participant's desire to learn computer skills in order to connect with other rural women. In addition, several rural women noted a desire to learn technical skills such as reading financial reports and writing grants and proposals. Urban women may have greater access to learning these skills through classes and contacts with other organizations or universities. It is possible that collaboration between rural and urban projects could allow for an exchange of resources and skills.

PLANNING FOR FUTURE INTERVENTIONS WITH WOMEN IN SUSTAINABLE DEVELOPMENT

Need for Case Studies

The most frequent suggestion for the forum curriculum was the inclusion of case studies, noted by 10 respondents. Generally, participants wanted to learn from others' successes, from the efforts of people "ahead of us." A male participant said he thought it would be helpful to learn about what women are doing in sustainable development and issues "specific to women." In addition, at least two women emphasized the importance of learning from others' mistakes. One participant said that she would like to take a "deeper and more detailed look" at what does and does not work, rather than restricting the focus to projects that, at least superficially, appear to be successful. Similarly, the director of a multi-issue political organization proposed the inclusion of honest discussions about what has not worked and why, as well as what was learned along the way.

The need for case studies expressed by these participants points to the lack of a sustainable development women's network. Many women may thus feel isolated in their efforts, not having clear role models and mentors. This isolation may be compounded for young women, women of color, or women who work predominantly with men. For example, a director of a tax reform organization explained that, as a young African American woman working with a mainly male board, "I do not always know where I am supposed to go." Not only was she forced to confront others' stereotypes, but she had to find her own way in an environment that offered little support. She pointed to the importance of networking, coalition building, and mentorship–women leaders guiding less experienced women leaders–as potential tools in reducing feelings of isolation.

Increased networking opportunities would also enable grassroots women to share with one another what they have learned from their experiences. In addition, formal collections and presentations of women's stories would enable women to feel more connected with the larger network, learn from others' efforts, and acknowledge women's contributions to development work.

Conceptualizations of Sustainable Development

As the interviewing process moved forward, it became clear that the term "sustainable development" was unfamiliar to some of the participants. This makes sense in light of the fact that it is generally an academic "buzzword," and there is no consistent conceptualization of the term. Unfortunately, use of terms such as this can create divisions between academic and grassroots women. Many women become involved in grassroots work because they are concerned about a specific issue. The intricacies of economic and sustainable development may seem obscure to them, and may prevent them from identifying themselves as actually working in sustainable development. For example, as a director of a domestic violence/employment center pointed out, women in service-oriented programs may be doing things in a sustainable way, but don't recognize it as "sustainable development." Several organizers in our sample fell into this category. For instance, the sewing factory (described above) donates scraps to the community development center for crafts projects. Similarly, the director of a mini-grant program described a project in which a garbage dump was transformed into a recreation area, and another in which a community center/day care was established in an abandoned school building. One respondent emphasized the importance of women educating themselves "to value what they already do," and to feel justified to "use the language."

Three respondents proposed discussing the definition(s) of sustainable development. In addition, many respondents had different views of sustainable development, or emphasized different components of the concept. One participant, for example, emphasized that sustainable development "connotes the idea of people working together, from all different walks of life." Another respondent wanted to consider "the assumptions behind sustainability." She questioned the accuracy of the "current mind set" that sustainability "requires growth," and wanted to look at sustainable agriculture on a small scale. A staff member of a social justice organization proposed a discussion of the "role of community organizing" in sustainable development, that is, finding a "niche for organizations whose work is in the political realm."

Finally, one participant discussed grassroots organizations that encourage a "sustainable development culture" (for example, "rejuvenating communities through storytelling"). As with organizers in service projects, he said that people involved in these organizations may not consider their work to be in the realm of sustainable development. Several projects in our sample did include this type of work. For example, one group directed a children's theater project in which the plays centered on social issues, while another project included a weekly African American history study group. Thus sustainable development includes a social and cultural component, which is often unrecognized.

Defining sustainable development is likely a dynamic process rather than an accomplishable concrete task. As sustainable development moves forward, and as social, environmental, and economic conditions change, the various definitions will evolve. However, discussing the meanings and implications behind sustainable development is crucial to reaching a degree of shared vision which, in turn, will enable players from all arenas to work together effectively, and thus create through their work newer and more involved definitions.

IMPLICATIONS

Clearly, grassroots development efforts in the southeastern United States encompass, in various ways, ideas of sustainable development. In addition, it appears that women are particularly attuned to the need for and potential success of sustainable development efforts, although many of them may not frame their work as sustainable development. There are also many characteristics specific to women's involvement in sustainable development. These include public health concerns, the ability to envision long-range solutions, and the complexities of working with men while maintaining leadership roles in organizations and in communities. Needs identified include lack of a strong network, need for education in technical and managerial skills, lack of resources such as credit and day care, lack of acceptance within the community, and family dynamics that may rigidify women's roles.

The research described here points to the importance of increased networking opportunities for women in sustainable development as a means of reducing isolation, sharing information and resources, and collaborating to move forward and break down barriers. In addition, increased communication between women from rural and urban areas will allow these two groups to envision and work towards common goals. Opportunities for open discussions between women and men are important to developing equal and compatible partnerships in sustainable development, and will also ensure that women's needs are fully represented in sustainable development work. Finally, networking can enable people from different areas to extensively share skills and resources; networking can facilitate, for example, communication among funders and academics as well as grassroots women. This process will also enable grassroots and academic women to bridge the gap between their worlds, so that they can develop a shared perspective and work toward common goals.

The 1996 Forum on Women, Community and Sustainable Development sponsored by the School of Social Work, Department of City and Regional Planning, and the University Center for International Studies at the University of North Carolina at Chapel Hill opened opportunities for collaboration and communication among men and women with different experiences from Asia, Africa, Latin America, and the southeastern United States. The Forum set the stage for a proposed annual training institute for grassroots women leaders and NGO representatives working in community sustainable development efforts. An evaluation of the Forum's effectiveness and participants' reactions will inform curriculum planning for the institute and will carry forward the research presented here.

REFERENCES

Absalom, E.O., Mwayaya, D., & Johnson, D. (1996). World neighbors in action: Learning with the community through Participatory Rural Appraisal. *A Newsletter for Project personnel, 24* (1E). Oklahoma City: World Neighbors.

Appleton, H., Fernandez, M.E., Hill, C.L.M., & Quiroz, C. (1995). Claiming and using indigenous knowledge. In U.N. Commission on Science and Technology Development, Gender Working Group. *Missing links: Gender equity in science and technology for development.* New York: United Nations Development Fund for Women.

Berry, T. (1988). *The dream of the earth.* San Francisco: Sierra Club Books.

Chambers, R. (1994). Participatory rural appraisal (PRA): Challenges, potential and paradigm. *World Development, 22*(10), pp. 1437-1454.

Creevey, L. (1996). *Changing women's lives and work: An analysis of the impacts of eight microenterprise projects.* London: Intermediate Technology Publications.

Daly, H.E. & Cobb, J.B., Jr. (1989). *For the Common Good: Redirecting the economy toward community, the environment, and a sustainable future.* Boston: Beacon Press.

Estes, R. (1993). Toward sustainable development: From theory to praxis. *Social development issues. 15*(3). pp. 1-29.

Gaventa, J. (1981). Land ownership in Appalachia, USA: A citizens' research project. In Dubell, Folke et al. (Eds.) *Research for the people, research by the people.* Linkoping, Sweden: Linkoping University, Dept. of Education. pp. 118-130.

Hall, B. (Ed.). 1988. *Environmental politics: Lessons from the grassroots.* Durham, NC: Institute for Southern Studies.

Harcourt, W. (Ed.). 1994. *Feminist perspectives on sustainable development.* London and New Jersey: ZED Books Ltd, in association with Rome: The Society For International Development.

Hinsdale, M.A., Lewis, H.M., & Waller, S. M. (1995). *It comes from the people: Community development and local theology.* Philadelphia, PA: Temple University Press.

Hoff, M.D. and McNutt, J.G. (Eds.) (1994). *The global environmental crisis: Implications for social welfare and social work.* Brookfield: Avebury.

Korten, D.C. (1995). *When corporations rule the world.* Co-publication of West Hartford, CT: Kumarian Press, Inc. & San Francisco, CA: Barrett-Koehler.

Leonard, A. (Ed.). (1995). *SEEDS 2: Supporting women's work around the world.* New York: The Feminist Press.

Marshall, C., & Rossman, G.B. (1995*). Designing qualitative research, second edition.* Thousand Oaks, CA: Sage Publications.

Noponen, H. (1996, May). *A gender analysis framework for understanding women's roles in sustainable development.* Paper presented at Women, community, and sustainable development: Collaborative approaches to skills theory, and practice, International Forum held at the University of North Carolina.

Patton, M.Q. (1987). *How to use qualitative methods in evaluation.* Newbury Park, CA: SAGE Publications.

Renshaw, L. (1995). Structural Adjustment. *Trialogue, 1*(1), p. 5.

United Nations Development Program (UNDP). (1996). *Human development report.* New York/Oxford: Oxford University Press.

UNIFEM (1993). UNIFEM Annual Report. New York: United Nations Development Fund for Women.

World Commission on Environment and Development (WCED). (1987). *Our common future: From one earth to one world.* New York: Oxford University Press.

Young, K. (1993*). Planning development with women: Making a world of difference.* New York: St. Martin's Press.

The Grameen Bank in Bangladesh:
Helping Poor Women
with Credit for Self-Employment

Golie G. Jansen, PhD
James L. Pippard, DSW

SUMMARY. Social work with poor women should include options for self-employment as avenues out of poverty. The Grameen Bank of Bangladesh exemplifies one micro-lending strategy to overcome traditional barriers and assist very poor women to earn an income and participate in the local economy. Credit lending principles combined with social development goals are highlighted, and the impact of this model discussed in terms of its success in alleviating poverty. Transferability of the model to the United States is discussed, and implications for social work offered. *[Article copies available for a fee from The Haworth Document Delivery Service: 1-800-342-9678. E-mail address: getinfo@haworthpressinc.com]*

POVERTY: DENIAL OF HUMAN RIGHTS

Social and economic policies worldwide increasingly reflect the withdrawal of governments' responsibilities for the poor. Concerns with basic

---

Golie G. Jansen is Assistant Professor, School of Social Work and Human Services, MS-19, 526 5th Street, Eastern Washington University, Cheney, WA 99004-2431 (E-mail: gjansen@ewu.edu).

James L. Pippard is Associate Professor, School of Social Work and Human Services, Eastern Washington University.

[Haworth co-indexing entry note]: "The Grameen Bank in Bangladesh: Helping Poor Women with Credit for Self-Employment." Jansen, Golie G., and James L. Pippard. Co-published simultaneously in *Journal of Community Practice* (The Haworth Press, Inc.) Vol. 5, No. 1/2, 1998, pp. 103-123; and: *Community Economic Development and Social Work* (ed: Margaret S. Sherraden, and William A. Ninacs) The Haworth Press, Inc., 1998, pp. 103-123. Single or multiple copies of this article are available for a fee from The Haworth Document Delivery Service [1-800-342-9678, 9:00 a.m. - 5:00 p.m. (EST). E-mail address: getinfo@haworthpressinc.com].

103

needs and human rights are losing ground to economic growth and greed. Muhammad Yunus, professor of economics and founder of the Grameen (meaning 'rural') Bank in Bangladesh, was visionary in drawing attention to poverty as a violation of human rights. He insisted that human rights violations are not limited to the denial of individual freedoms, but occur when people lack basic needs, such as food, shelter, health and education (Yunus, 1987). His vision is captured in article 25 (1) of the United Nations Universal Declaration of Human Rights:

> Everyone has the right to a standard of living adequate for the health and well being of himself (sic) and his family, including food, clothing, housing and medical care, and necessary social services, and the right to security in the event of unemployment, sickness, disability, widowhood, old age or other lack of livelihood in circumstances beyond his (sic) control. (UN General Assembly, 1948, In Yunus, 1987, p. 1)

Yunus believes that credit for self-employment represents a fundamental human right; without economic resources all other human rights cannot be realized. This conviction was instrumental in the development of the Grameen Bank, which pioneered a peer-lending banking approach geared toward improving the human rights of mainly poor women. The Grameen Bank seeks to empower people to overcome the oppressive conditions of exploitation, poverty, and ignorance. The Bank provides credit without collateral to the poorest of the poor who have no assets, and assists poor women to escape extreme poverty. By owning a little, a poor woman achieves a sense of economic and personal autonomy, which is a significant improvement over owning nothing at all.

The purpose of this article is to exemplify the Grameen Bank of Bangladesh as one model of microenterprise development in addressing women's economic and social development needs. The article first discusses gender inequities in women's economic participation as a context for understanding the significance of the Grameen Bank for poor women. Then it discusses positive effects and critiques of the Bank, as well as the appeal and application of this model in the United States. Finally, the article offers practice implications for social workers.

PERSISTING INEQUALITIES: WOMEN IN ECONOMIC DEVELOPMENT

Women compose one-half of the world's population and perform two-thirds of the world's work hours, yet are everywhere poorer in resources and poorly represented in positions of decision making power. (Peterson & Runyan, 1993, p. 5)

In the 1970s, international development agencies confronted the importance of the role of women in economic development. At that time, evaluations of economic development programs revealed increasing inequality between men and women. It was found that the introduction of cash crops and modern technology decreased the significance of women's roles in food production and thus their relative equality with men in terms of access to economic resources (Boserup, 1970). Boserup's findings challenged the long held notions that the position of women automatically improves with economic development. As a result, women engaged in development work took action and framed a 'Women in Development' agenda, promoting women's interest in development in terms of economic justice and not just as an issue of social equality. Gender differences as a factor in resource allocation became a major field of activism, policy, and research (Sen & Grown, 1987; Tinker, 1990).

Through the United Nations Decade for Women and three International Women's Conferences–Mexico City, 1975; Nairobi, 1985; and Beijing, 1995–women have advanced this economic justice agenda and also claimed recognition for their social and economic contributions (Young, 1993). Indeed, during the last two decades women made gains in terms of health, education, and political participation, while in many countries violence against women is now considered a violation of human rights (Kerr, 1993; Young, 1993). Yet the exclusive focus on the above social gains ignores the economic realities of women's lives–women's relative access to economic resources dropped during that same time, and their income and employment worsened while their workload increased (Sen & Grown, 1987).

Through increased data collection and availability of women's experiences in the global economy, development activists and policy makers recognize these enduring inequalities as global feminist issues. Data from the United Nations and other sources reveal that women earn 10% of the world's income and represent one percent of property owners. Of the 1.3 billion people living in poverty, 70% are women (Peterson & Runyan, 1993). Worldwide, women's income is lower than that of men, yet while women tend to spend their income on family needs men put personal needs first (Jacobson, 1992; Millar & Glendinning, 1989). In developing countries the absence of reproductive rights (i.e., family planning and birth control) contributes to high birthrates and poverty (Jacobson, 1992). In addition, restrictions on land ownership and access to credit curtail women's economic independence and success making women poorer than men (Jacobson, 1992; United Nations, 1991). Thus, women still are the most poor, the most illiterate, and the most disenfranchised. In fact, throughout the 1980s national debts and structural adjustment policies disproportionately affected women in terms of access to food, healthcare, educational status, and housing (Sen & Grown, 1987; Young, 1993).

Intending to address these disadvantages of women, governments and international development organizations in the 1970s and 1980s started to involve women in macroeconomic and health and welfare participatory development projects as a matter of policy (Mayoux, 1995). Governments and organizations believed that by involving women in development, their social and economic position would improve. Although progressive at the time, currently these approaches are evaluated as failing to address poor women's concerns about improving their economic status (Mayoux, 1995). Researchers found that women working a full day rarely could participate in development; and if they did, "the relationship between women's time and resource input and the benefits they enjoy is generally mediated by the power relations within the household and the community" (Mayoux, 1995, p. 248). Men often oppose women's involvement when activities are not in their interest (Andreas, 1985; Carney, 1992). Men promote cash crops and mechanization, while women may be more interested in food crops, appropriate technology, and planting trees for fuel or food processing and storage (Sen & Grown, 1987). Unless the underlying aspects of traditional gender-based subordination of women (such as rights to productive resources, gender division of labor, and violence against women) are addressed with conscious empowerment strategies, participatory development efforts are not sufficient. "The evidence suggests that gender inequalities in resources, time availability, and power influence the activities, priorities, and framework of participatory projects just as much as 'top-down' development and market activities" (Mayoux, 1995, p. 235). Conclusions like these suggest that the solution to women's economic dependency is not just participation, but requires ". . . a linking with wider movements for change in the national and international development agenda" (Mayoux, 1995, p. 235) to promote "women's control over their own economic decisions and over policies that affect these decisions" (Sen & Grown, 1987, p. 82).

Microenterprise programs address some of these concerns and increasingly are considered viable strategies to reduce poverty. These credit lending programs offer unique opportunities to poor women by challenging class and gender inequities in economic opportunities (Berger, 1989; Raheim & Bolden, 1995). Designed as grass roots initiatives and modeled after projects in the developing world, these initiatives recognize women's systematic exclusion from training, technical assistance, and capital access (Raheim, 1996). Microenterprise development projects address these disadvantages. They offer credit and other services to create and sustain self-employment that provides an adequate income for poor women. The Grameen Bank of Bangladesh pioneered one of the most prominent peer-lending models of microenterprise development and has "become an international 'icon' for organizations that foster micro-enterprises in the service of the poor" (Auwal, 1996, p. 28). The relevance of the Grameen Bank for this country lies in the fact that a significant number of micro-lending projects in the United States are designed after this peer-lending model.

THE GRAMEEN BANK: CREDIT FOR POOR WOMEN

Socioeconomic Context

Bangladesh, formerly East Pakistan, gained independence in 1971 after an extremely violent liberation struggle and civil war. An estimated one to three million Bangladeshi were killed and many families uprooted and made homeless. The devastation of civil war was followed by a short-lived "euphoria to create a dreamland for 75 million people" (Yunus, 1994a, p. 3). A major flood caused economic collapse, followed by severe famine in 1974 (Wahid, 1993; Yunus, 1994a). Hundreds of thousands of people died. In order to survive, many poor farmers borrowed heavily and ultimately lost their land and belongings to moneylenders who charged excessive interest rates (Food & Agricultural Organization, 1987). Landlessness became a serious problem: in 1979, 48.7% of rural households owned less than one-half acre of land (Hossain, 1988). They were considered landless because households cannot produce an adequate income from such a small plot (Wahid, 1993). Poor rural women were especially affected by these natural and socioeconomic disasters of the 1970s, as poverty and hunger affect women more seriously than men (Yunus, 1987).

Cultural Context: Women in Bangladesh

Poor rural women represent the most vulnerable group in Bangladesh—they are isolated and deprived (Schuler & Hashemi, 1995). Although women contribute considerably to rural economic activities, women gain neither recognition nor status from their work (Abdullah & Zeidenstein, 1982). They do not own land, are not allowed to be educated, and are socialized to think of themselves as being inferior to men (Papa, Auwal, & Singhal, 1995). Their usually arranged marriages occur when they are very young, often long before puberty. The tradition of dowry, although illegal, contributes to the view that daughters are a burden to poor families (Papa, Auwal, & Singhal, 1995). At marriage they move into the household compound of their husbands. They work long hours and are bound by traditional roles and the system of 'purdah,' "a system for the seclusion of women" (Khan, 1988, p. 33). A strict Muslim doctrine, 'purdah' requires Bangladeshi women to be completely veiled in public. They are not allowed out of the family enclave, and many women may never visit local towns only a few miles away from their homes (Auwal, 1996). Most Bangladeshi women stay out of the paid labor force. If a family is poor and cannot feed all of its members, an unwritten law requires the wife, sister, or mother to forego food and starve, leading to a higher mortality rate for women than for men (Shehabuddin, 1992). The extreme poverty as a result of floods and famine and its effects on already isolated and deprived women frames the genesis of the Grameen Bank.

History of the Grameen Bank

> If we are looking for one single action which will enable the poor to overcome their poverty, I would go for credit. Money is power. (Yunus, 1994a, p. 9)

In 1974 when thousands of Bangladeshi died of hunger, Dr. Yunus, Chairman of the Economics Department at Chittagong University, found little use for the economic theories he had studied at Vanderbilt University in Tennessee. He decided to learn about the lives of poor people in the countryside surrounding the University:

> I met a woman, Sophia, who made bamboo stools. She was extremely poor. No wonder she was poor. She made only two pennies US$ a day by making bamboo stools. Why so little? Because she did not have the working capital to buy bamboo from the market for 20 pennies US$. A trader lent her the money with the condition that she would sell her product to him at the price he decides. Now you can guess why she was extremely poor. (Yunus, 1994a, pp. 3-4)

He observed blatant exploitation of poor women by money-lenders. Women were paying up to 10% a day on their loans, keeping them from making reasonable gains from their work. Yunus concluded that cheap and accessible credit was key to combating poverty for Sophia and others like her. He found 42 other people who, if they were to cut out the lender, collectively only needed 30 dollars. When Yunus approached a traditional bank, he was informed that poor people had no right to credit. The bank explained that:

> Banks need collateral. The poor cannot offer collateral. Moreover, the poor are not to be trusted. They are not credit worthy. Banking is a business. It cannot indulge in charity for the poor. (Yunus, 1994a, p. 5)

Dr. Yunus was convinced that "if financial resources are made available to the poor at reasonable terms and conditions, they can generate productive self-employment without external assistance" (Hossain, 1988, p. 23). By presenting himself as the loan guarantor, the bank agreed to make the loan. Thus, the Grameen Bank began in 1976 as a small loan project with the following objectives:

> (1) to extend banking facilities to poor women and men; (2) to eliminate the exploitation of money-lenders; (3) to create opportunities for self-employment for the vast unutilized and under-utilized labor resource; (4) to bring the disadvantaged people within the folds of some organizational format which they can understand, operate, and in which they can find socio-political and economic strength through mutual support; and (5) to reverse the age-old vicious cycle of "low income, low savings, low investment, low income" into an expanding system of "low income, credit, investment, more income, more credit, more investment, more income. (Yunus, 1982, p. 11)

The initial loan project was a success and in 1979, Dr. Yunus launched the Grameen Bank as an action/research project with support of local banks and the Bangladesh Central Bank. The average loans were the equivalent of US$66 with a repayment record of 98%. Within a year, 24 rural branches were opened. In 1983, the government passed an ordinance transforming the project into an independent specialized bank for the poor with an authorized capital of US$2.8 million (Hossain, 1988).

The Grameen Bank is participatory and empowerment based. It is a financial institution and a social development organization for, of, and by the poor (Auwal, 1996). From the very outset the Bank was designed to be owned and controlled by the people who borrow from it. Each borrower owns a mandatory share, which costs three US dollars. In 1994, 92% of the Bank was owned by its borrowers, while eight percent was owned by the government. As of February, 1995, the Bank has dispersed more than one billion US dollars in loans to the poor and serves over two million borrowers. Of the borrowers, 95% are women (Auwal, 1996). The initial annual loan is as small as US$10 or $15, with an average loan size of US$100. The simple interest rate is 20% on principal amounts and the repayment rate is 99% (Auwal, 1996).

The borrowers are mandatory savers and the total savings of all Grameen borrowers in 1994 was in excess of US$70 million (Yunus, 1994a). Since 1984 the Grameen Bank has offered housing loans with an average size of US$300 to be repaid in ten years. So far, 350,000 houses have been built from these loans (Yunus, 1994a, 1994b).

In 1994, the Grameen Bank had over one thousand branch offices serving 34,000 villages; half of all villages operated by 11,631 staff members (Yunus, 1994a). Because of its intensive and expansive micro-organization approach, the Grameen Bank long depended on subsidies from international donors, such as the International Fund for Agricultural Development. Recently it sold US$163 million in bonds to six commercial banks in Bangladesh and has for the first time gained independence from outside donor agencies (Kane, 1996). Addressing Canadian bankers in 1996, Dr. Yunus stated: "Today we issue bonds, raise money, and take care of all our expenses with our own income, last year lending over US$400 million, which exceeded the combined total of rural loans made by all banks in Bangladesh ("Missionaries of micro-credit," 1996, p. 30).

Basic Organizing Principles of the Grameen Bank

The basic principle of the Grameen Bank is that credit is a human right. The Grameen Bank set out to prove that lending to the poor is a viable proposition, and that when given credit, poor people have opportunities to escape poverty. The unique approach of the Bank lies in its combination of economic and social development goals. Grameen-style banking is characterized by providing credit without collateral through peer lending groups, and by taking the bank to the poor. This is a very different approach from traditional banking. Traditional bankers believe that the poor are a credit risk, that they cannot budget and will not save, and assert that poor women in particular have no skills. Through its approach, the Grameen Bank actively dismisses common stereotypes of the poor. The following elements of the Grameen Bank exemplify these approaches: (1) Non-traditional target group; (2) Peer-lending through solidarity groups; (3) Bank goes to the poor; (4) Pyramid organizational structure; (5) Social development combined with economic development; (6) Intensive training of bank workers and borrowers; and (7) Savings requirement. All these elements represent a grassroots community organizing model–they engage people actively in their own and others' economic and social lives.

Non-Traditional Target Group

The Grameen Bank primarily serves the poorest of the poor—only those who own less than half an acre of farmland qualify for credit without collateral. Because of the gender biased banking system, women were given priority to get loans (Yunus, 1994b) and today 95% of the borrowers are poor, illiterate women (Auwal, 1996). The Grameen Bank believes that poor people do not need to be literate to engage in banking, and with access to capital they will know what to do. Women are more active, more frugal, and more successful than men in running small businesses, suggesting "that if women are properly approached . . . they are actually ready to respond appropriately" (Wahid, 1993, p. 37). In addition, women generally use the money for household needs and capital improvement and are less likely to squander funds (Counts, 1996; Kamaluddin, 1993).

Peer-Lending Through Solidarity Groups

The Grameen Bank pioneered an innovative peer-lending credit model. Since poor women have no collateral to obtain loans, they are organized in 'solidarity' groups of no more than five persons. Women in other countries now use the peer-lending concept to obtain credit for starting microenterprises (Tinker, 1990). Solidarity groups form the core of the Grameen Bank. Much thought is given to the size and function of the groups:

> Before asking the group to guarantee loans to individual members, it is imperative to foster a sense of group solidarity. This is done by keeping the groups small, by having as members only persons of similar socioeconomic status and sex, and by encouraging both individual and community improvement objectives, which range from reducing family size or refusing to pay dowries, to improving community water supplies. (Tinker, 1990, p. 39)

In the Grameen Bank, only one household member can be part of any group, and relatives cannot join that group. Each group elects a chairperson and a secretary on a yearly rotating basis, so that each learns leadership roles. A new group of borrowers is required to participate in a training of at least seven days to learn about the Grameen philosophy, banking rules and procedures, business skills, the responsibilities of the group chairperson, and the group savings program. They are also taught about health, children's education, other social development programs, and how to sign their names (Hossain, 1993). After the training each group attends weekly meetings. When the group demonstrates familiarity with the rules and regulations, formal status is granted. Loans are given to two members first, and if repayment is made according to schedule each week for at least two months, the next two members become eligible. The money must be used immediately for productive activity and paid back in 50 weekly installments. The chairperson, responsible for loan repayment of group members, is the last to receive a loan. If one member cannot repay her loan, none of the group members will be eligible for future loans. The loans are used for an enormous range of activities: women make pots, raise poultry, cows and goats, make and sell handicrafts such as mats and baskets, grow fruits and vegetables, husk paddy and puff rice (Shehabuddin, 1992). Solidarity groups offer advantages over individual loan programs in that group members act (1) as support to undertake business risks not taken as an individual; (2) as support/pressure group to monitor and guarantee individual loan repayment schedules; and (3) as personal and social support for each other.

The Bank Goes to the Poor

The Grameen Bank has a 'user friendly' and culturally appropriate structure and thus appeals to women who are shy in public places and are not used to going to banks. "With Grameen the poor do not have to come to the Bank, instead, the Bank goes to the poor" (Shams, 1992, p. 9). The link between the bank and 'solidarity' group is a highly trained community development worker, called a bank worker, who must live in the village. Bank workers recruit women, organize solidarity groups, conduct training, and participate in the weekly center meetings. Each bank worker is responsible for about 250 borrowers.

Pyramid Organizational Structure

The Grameen Bank is a decentralized, pyramidal banking structure including lending units, centers, branch offices, area offices, and a head office in Dacca. At the village level, solidarity groups are the basic lending units. Eight groups constitute a center, while 30-60 centers represent a branch. Each center elects a chief from the groups' chairpersons. Group members are required to attend weekly center meetings conducted by the center chief who oversees applications for new loans as well as payment of loan installments. The bank worker attends all meetings, participates in the discussions, and disburses and receives money. Thus banking is conducted openly in front of all members, and members take active roles in discussions on progress and problems. "This provides the opportunity for members to become informed, involved, and to assess their own performance in comparison to others" (Islam, Wahid, & Khan, 1993, p. 31). The structure of the Grameen Bank is thus foremost a grassroots organizing approach, facilitating participation and the development of leadership skills.

Social Development Goals: "The Sixteen Decisions"

The Grameen Bank is not solely a financial institution. In March, 1984, a national workshop of 100 female branch managers formulated the "Sixteen Decisions," which added a social development program to the Grameen Bank (Hossain, 1993). The "Sixteen Decisions" are a blueprint for action with the goal of improved health and living standards. The Grameen bank "is perhaps the only bank in the world that encourages birth control, sanitation and a clean environment as part of its lending policy" (Kamaluddin, 1993, p. 38). The result of this focus is that many poor families whose members are often ill and uneducated are given the opportunity to better their lives on every level. Members are taught and expected to live by these principles (Hossain, 1993):

1. The four principles of Grameen Bank–discipline, unity, courage, and hard work–we shall follow and advance in all walks of our lives.
2. We shall bring prosperity to our families.
3. We shall not live in dilapidated houses. We shall repair our houses and work toward constructing new houses as soon as possible.
4. We shall grow vegetables all year round. We shall eat plenty of them and sell surplus.
5. During planting seasons, we shall plant as many seedlings as possible.
6. We shall plan to keep our families small. We shall minimize our expenditures. We shall look after our health.
7. We shall educate our children and ensure that they can earn enough to pay for their education.
8. We shall always keep our children and the environment clean.
9. We shall build and use pit latrines.
10. We shall drink tube well water. If it is not available, we shall boil water or use alum.
11. We shall not take any dowry in our sons' weddings, neither shall we give any dowry in our daughters' weddings. We shall keep the center free from the curse of dowry. We shall not practice child marriage.

12. We shall not inflict any injustice on anyone, neither shall we allow anyone to do so.
13. For higher income we shall collectively undertake bigger investments.
14. We shall always be ready to help each other. If anyone is in difficulty, we shall all help.
15. If we come to know of any breach of discipline in any center, we shall all go there and help restore discipline.
16. We shall introduce physical exercise in all our centers. We shall take part in all social activities collectively.

Intensive Training of Bank Workers and Borrowers

As part of its empowerment philosophy the Grameen Bank gives high priority to educating and training its bank personnel and borrowers. The bank's success is attributed to the quality of its staff (Jain, 1996; MacIsaac & Wahid, 1993). The goal of the training is to build committed bank employees who work in accordance with the bank's philosophy. Prospective branch managers, who are recent university graduates, are trained for six months–five months extensive fieldwork practice in a branch office, and 4 weeks in-class study. Trainees learn about banking procedures such as loan processing, deposit-banking, record keeping, and accounts maintenance. Trainees also study group dynamics and life histories. Trainees must complete two detailed case studies of borrowers and how the bank has made a difference in their lives. This assignment resembles qualitative interviewing, as trainees describe the story from the borrower's point of view and refrain from interpreting the facts. This exercise orients the bank worker to the poverty of rural life and how the poor perceive the bank (MacIsaac & Wahid, 1993). Each trainee visits at least 15 different centers before being assigned to a branch. The branch managers in turn are responsible for training bank workers. In addition, center chiefs and bank personnel attend periodic workshops to exchange new ideas and share experiences (Hossain, 1993).

In addition, the bank organizes numerous workshops for borrowers on national, area and branch levels. Each borrower must participate in one intense seven day branch level workshop to discuss achievements, future plans, and the "Sixteen Decisions." Other workshop topics include health, nutrition, family planning, and other women's issues. Women also visit other area centers and projects, and learn about new schools, sanitation, and drinking water provisions. Participants are expected to organize a one-day 'mini-workshop' in their villages to present what they learned. The philosophy of these workshops is to train all women in leadership skills, to allow all to participate in decision-making, and not to create a small group that gains power over the rest (Shehabuddin, 1992).

Savings Requirement

Grameen Bank regulations require borrowers to save. Each borrower saves 2.5 cents a week in addition to five percent of the loan money. The savings go into a Group Fund which is used for interest free emergency loans in case of death of a family member or a cow, or damage to equipment. The Group Fund is controlled by the group and gives members an essential experience in consensual, collective financial management. The Group Fund moneys are saved in the Grameen Bank at an 8.5% annual interest rate. The total savings of all Grameen borrowers is in excess of $70 million (Hossain, 1993; Yunus, 1994a).

These Grameen Bank activities for women are a big departure from their previously secluded lives; therefore, participating in the Grameen Bank is not without risks. Many women face criticism from husbands and other men who are threatened by their independence. Some women fear that they violate religious principles and others are scared to manage money on their own. Thus, belonging to an organization with strong convictions is a vital element for personal growth.

IMPACT OF THE GRAMEEN BANK

> None of the poverty programs has yet proven to be so successful in drawing the attention of its target group in the history of Bangladesh. The success of the Grameen Bank on this front may be attributable to its innovative approach, participatory management style, rigorous counseling, and close supervision of the members' activities and, above all, the sincere devotion and commitment of the well-trained bank workers. (Wahid, 1993, p. 36)

The success of the unconventional banking style of the Grameen Bank is well documented (Hossain, 1988; Mizan, 1993; Rahman & Islam, 1993; Wahid, 1993, 1994). The success of the Grameen Bank's loan recovery has to do with peer pressure and solidarity, income producing loans, a repayment scheme that requires weekly installments, availability of emergency loans, the great dedication of bank workers, and a conscious philosophy about the social change and the role of women (Jain, 1996; Rahman & Islam, 1993; Tinker, 1989). The Grameen Bank has generated new employment and productivity. In 1993, an independent evaluation found that "among women who had been borrowing from the Grameen for eight or more years, 46% had crossed above the poverty line and had accumulated enough assets to be unlikely to fall below it . . . Among non Grameen families only four percent had come out of poverty over the same period of time" (Counts, 1996, p. xiv). Papa, Auwal, and Singhal (1995) found the Grameen Bank perceived as a 'life line' for the borrowers because it provided "their escape from poverty, vulnerability and socioeconomic injustice" (p. 211).

The success goes far beyond economic success. Especially in terms of women's participation in economic activities, the Grameen Bank has "revolutionized the rural people's attitude toward women and work" (Wahid, 1994, p. 5). Women's involvement in the bank contributed in major ways to their emancipation, their decreased economic dependence on men, and their increased decision-making power and status in the family (Mizan, 1993; Schuler & Hashemi, 1995). Also, women are empowered by establishing an identity outside their families and gaining confidence in operating in the public sphere (Hashemi, Schuler, & Riley, 1996). In addition, women are becoming leaders for the first time in their lives (Ashe & Cosslett, 1989). Participation in the Grameen Bank was found to have significant effects on levels of contraceptive use (Schuler & Hashemi, 1995) while the nutritional status of Grameen participants is higher than that of non-borrowers, as is the per capita spending on health and education (Rahman & Islam, 1993).

The Grameen Bank, through its focus on credit, successfully demonstrates that landless poor women can improve their economic and personal lives within the context of group solidarity and a larger social development agenda (Hashemi, Schuler, & Riley, 1996; Tinker, 1989).

Critique

The Grameen Bank is not without its critics who find fault with both the model and its execution. Leftists and feminists have criticized the Grameen Bank for its 'minimalist' approach, which fails to address larger redistributive issues such as land reform (Counts, 1996) and redistribution of power in the household (Ebdon, 1995; Goetz & Sen Gupta, 1994). Others express concern that a focus on microlending programs moves the responsibility for anti-poverty programs to poor people themselves (Neff, 1996) and may obscure the continued need for structural development programs and policies that address the full integration of women (Berger, 1989; Van der Wees & Romijn, 1995). Liberal economists criticize the use of money for household expenditures rather than for business growth and expansion (Tinker, 1989), thus raising questions whether a microenterprise program such as the Grameen Bank would improve opportunities for economic upward mobility (Novogratz, 1992; Rahman, 1993).

Critics of the execution of the model question whether credit programs for women actually challenge gender inequality in the household, and whether the goal of empowerment suffers from a focus on performance. In terms of gender inequality, Goetz and Sen Gupta (1994) frequently found that women hand over the loans to their husbands, and only receive enough money to make weekly payments. In cases of default, women suffer the consequence because loans are in their names. The results are tense gender relations and even incidents of domestic violence (Ebdon, 1995). Ebdon (1995) quotes Hashemi and Schuler (1992), who found evidence that Grameen Bank workers "creamed" borrowers with existing incomes or assets, so that repayments would be guaranteed. Ebdon (1995) criticizes the performance-driven approach, which endangers the participatory and empowerment objectives. She observed bank workers who focused exclusively on loan repayments and savings when meeting with groups of women, without engaging them in solidarity-building and self-development through education and consciousness-raising. Credit-worthiness rather than poverty alleviation, according to Ebdon, excluded the very poorest women and weakened the ideal of empowerment.

WORLDWIDE APPEAL AND REPLICABILITY OF THE GRAMEEN MODEL

The Grameen Bank's conviction that credit is a human right inspired peer lending banking models in over 70 countries (Auwal, 1996). Through the visibility and success of the Grameen Bank, microenterprise programs increasingly are considered viable strategies to reduce poverty in both developing countries and the United States. The application of the model has been successful in countries such as Kenya, the Philippines, Ethiopia, and Malaysia (Kamaluddin, 1993). Although many of these microcredit programs use the peer lending model, competing credit lending models exist (for a typology and examples of international credit programs for women, see Berger, 1989; Dignard & Havet, 1995).

As the Grameen Bank has positively contributed to the alleviation of poverty for the poorest of the poor in Bangladesh, replicability to the United States often raises questions. Starting a small business in Bangladesh–selling eggs or baskets–in the informal sector without welfare as an alternative income support is different from starting a small business in the United States. Business start ups in this country require more than $100 and potential entrepreneurs are faced with more bureaucratic complexities.

In addition, cultural differences influence conceptualization and practices of how to run a business (Auwal, 1996). For instance, Mondal and Tune (1993) identified factors different from American culture that are conducive to the structure of the Grameen Bank: homogeneity in religion (Islam), the structure of poverty, group identity, and respect for authority. Regardless of these differences, the appeal of the Grameen Bank is tremendous as it exemplifies access to credit and training for poor people that are not usually considered a good credit risk for business development. The goals of increased individual economic independence combined with strong program and peer support, seems to be a successful formula for people in communities that are not part of the economic mainstream.

Microenterprise programs for low income women in the United States emerged in the 1980s under different auspices and with funds from different public and private sources (for an overview, see Else & Raheim, 1992; Raheim, 1996, 1997; Raheim & Bolden, 1995). Many of these programs adopted the organizing strategies of the Grameen Bank (Else & Raheim, 1992; Gugliotta, 1993). Early examples of these programs are the urban Women's Self-Employment Project "Full Circle Fund" in Chicago and the rural "Good Faith Fund" in Pine Bluff, Arkansas, both developed in 1988. Projects for self-employment have seen a tremendous growth. In 1996 there were over 266 programs in 46 states that assisted over 36,000 businesses and loaned more than $126 million (Severens and Kays, 1997). Early assessments of these programs indicate success (Clark & Huston, 1993; Raheim, 1996). Clark and Huston (1993) found that microenterprises not only support owner-operators, but more than half employed at least one employee and some two or three. Not only is economic success evident, but studies indicate women gained a sense of autonomy, as well as improved family relationships as part of these economic opportunities (Clark & Huston, 1993; Gowdy & Pearlmutter; 1993; Raheim, 1996; Raheim & Bolden, 1995), findings not unlike those documented about women participants of the Grameen Bank.

IMPLICATIONS FOR SOCIAL WORK

The Grameen Bank sets an example for grass roots economic and social development. This credit lending scheme and social development program successfully mobilizes poor, illiterate women into groups and teaches them to plan, cooperate, generate income, and to carry collective responsibilities. Each success is a collective success and women together improve their lives and that of their families. The major success of the Grameen Bank is reaching their target group (poor, isolated women) with credit lending opportunities and highly committed workers who have intense contact with the participants.

Social work's concern about poor women in the United States has focused mainly on the feminization of poverty and social welfare policies (Abramovitz, 1989; Miller, 1990) related to residual welfare reform and welfare-to-work policies (Hagen, 1992; Hagen & Lurie, 1995; Rosenthal, 1994; Segal, 1989). These conventional, remedial programs–with a focus on transfer payments and job training for poor women–are not successful in helping women achieve economic self-sufficiency. Wage labor, especially for women who are poor, single mothers, will not lift them out of poverty (Gueron & Pauli, 1991; Miller, 1990; U.S. General Accounting Office, 1993). In addition, many welfare recipients and former welfare recipients faced with the need to find work are unsuccessful despite the current requirements of the Personal Responsibility and Work Opportunity Reconciliation Act of 1996.

One alternative to wage labor is self employment and some policymakers promote this as a solution to gain economic independence. However, just as in Bangladesh, major barriers exist for low income women and welfare recipients to pursue self-employment. They face similar personal obstacles: lack of access to capital, lack of business knowledge and skills, low self-esteem, and lack of confidence. In addition, they face structural barriers inherent in social welfare policy (Raheim, 1997).

The growing microenterprise development movement in the U.S. should appeal to social workers interested in promoting economic self-sufficiency. The role of social workers is to participate in innovative and creative community practice approaches that promote self-employment projects as an alternative or supplement to welfare (Midgley, 1996; Raheim, 1997; Raheim & Bolden, 1995). In addition, social workers should advocate for policy changes that reduce barriers for TANF recipients to start a business (Raheim, 1997).

Now more than ever, social workers should join with Muhammed Yunus in his conviction that poverty is a denial of human rights. With access to knowledge, skills, and credit, as well as supportive policies, microlending and self-employment programs can be successful for specific interested groups of poor and unemployed women as a way out of poverty. However, micro-enterprise programs are only a small solution to urban poverty and should be part of an overall strategy of poverty alleviation. Bates and Servon (1996) urge us to understand the microenterprise movement in its proper perspective. They observe that:

> Policy makers and the media have bought into the idea that small loans to poor minorities can serve as bootstraps: the ghetto dweller

> can open a small business and achieve affluence, creating jobs for the other inner-city residents in the process. While it is true that microenterprise loans do create jobs, the loans are not large enough, nor are there enough of them to revitalize poor communities. (p. 27)

Social workers should be mindful that success of microlending should be understood as only a partial answer to poverty alleviation. Social justice goals should never be unrelated to work for economic self-sufficiency as Rahman (1993) suggests: "the Grameen Bank model cannot be the answer to the poverty created by an unjust socioeconomic and political structure. A favorable policy regime, followed by a desirable political change at the macro structure, is the precondition for successful initiation and sustenance of a Grameen Bank-type of program for poverty alleviation" (p. 217).

REFERENCES

Abdullah, T., & Zeidenstein, S. A. (1982). *Village women of Bangladesh: Prospects for change.* Oxford: Pergamon Press.

Abramovitz, M. (1989). *Regulating the lives of women: Social welfare policy from colonial times to the present.* Boston: South End Press.

Andreas, C. (1985). *When women rebel: The rise of popular feminism in Peru.* Westport, CT: Lawrence Hill & Co.

Ashe, J., & Cosslett, C. (1989). *Credit for the poor: Past activities and future directions for the United Nations Development Programme.* New York: Policy Division Bureau for Programme Policy and Evaluation, UNDP.

Auwal, M. A. (1996). Promoting microcapitalism in the service of the poor: The Grameen model and its cross-cultural adaptation. *The Journal of Business Communication, 33*(1), 27-49.

Bates, T.M., & Servon, L. (1996). Why loans won't save the poor. *Inc., 18*(5), 27-28.

Berger, M. (1989). The strengths and limitations of credit as a tool for alleviating poverty. *World Development, 17*(7), 1017-1032.

Boserup, E. (1970). *Women's role in economic development.* New York: St. Martin's Press.

Carney, J.A. (1992). Peasant women and economic transformation in the Gambia. *Development and Change, 23*(3), 67-90.

Clark, P., & Huston, T. (1993). *Assisting the smallest businesses: Assessing microenterprise development as a strategy for boosting poor communities, an interim report.* Washington, DC: Aspen Institute.

Counts, A. (1996). *Give us credit.* New York: Random House.

Dignard, L., & Havet, J. (1995). *Women in micro- and small-scale enterprise development.* Boulder, CO: Westview Press.

Directory for Microenterprise Development. (1996). *The self-employment learning project.* Washington, DC: Aspen Institute.

Ebdon, R. (1995). NGO expansion and the fight to reach the poor: Gender implications of NGO scaling up in Bangladesh. *IDS Bulletin, 26*(3), 49-55.

Else, J. F., & Raheim, S. (1992). AFDC clients as entrepreneurs: Self employment offers an important option. *Public Welfare, 50*(4), 36-41.

Food and Agricultural Organization. (1987). *The paradigm of communication in development: From knowledge transfer to community participation, lessons from Grameen Bank, Bangladesh.* Rome: FAO of the United Nations.

Goetz, A.M., & Sen Gupta, R. (1994, September). *Who takes the credit? Gender, power and control over loan use in rural credit programmes in Bangladesh.* Unpublished manuscript, Brighton, UK: Institute of Development Studies, University of Sussex.

Gowdy, E.A., & Pearlmutter, S. (1993). Economic self-sufficiency: It's not just money. *Affilia, 8*(4), 368-387.

Gueron, J. M., & Pauli, E. (1991). *From welfare to work.* New York: Russell Sage Foundation.

Gugliotta, G. (1993, May 6). Microenterprise is growing. *The Washington Post*, p. A1.

Hagen, J. L. (1992). Women, work and welfare: Is there a role for social work? *Social Work, 37*(1), 9-14.

Hagen, J. L., & Lurie, I. (1995). Implementing JOBS: From the rose garden to reality. *Social Work, 40*(4), 523-532.

Hashemi, S.M., & Schuler, S.R. (1992, June). *State and NGO support networks in rural Bangladesh: Conflicts and coalitions for control* (Working Paper). Dhaka, Bangladesh: Development Research Center.

Hashemi, S.M., Schuler, S.R., & Riley, A.P. (1996). Rural credit programs and women's empowerment in Bangladesh. *World Development, 24*(4), 635-653.

Hossain, M. (1988). Credit for alleviation of rural poverty: *The Grameen Bank in Bangladesh. International Food Policy Institute, 65,* 23-32.

Hossain, M. (1993). The Grameen Bank: Its origin, organization and management style. In A. N. M. Wahid (Ed.), *The Grameen Bank. Poverty relief in Bangladesh* (pp. 9-23). Boulder, CO: Westview Press.

Islam, M. M., Wahid, A. N. M., & Khan, Z. H. (1993). The Grameen Bank: Peer monitoring in a dual credit market. In A.N.M. Wahid (Ed.), *The Grameen Bank. Poverty relief in Bangladesh* (pp. 23-33). Boulder, CO: Westview Press.

Jacobson, J.L. (1992). *Gender bias: Roadblock to sustainable development.* Washington, DC: Worldwatch Institute.

Jain, P.S. (1996). Managing credit for the rural poor: Lessons from the Grameen Bank. *World Development, 24*(1), 79-89.

Kamaluddin, S. (1993, March 18). Lender with a mission. Bangladesh's Grameen Bank targets poorest of the poor. *Far Eastern Economic Review, 156* (11), 38-40.

Kane, H. (1996, March/April). Micro-enterprise. *Worldwatch, 9,* 10-19.

Kerr, J. (1993). (Ed.). *Ours by right: Women's rights as human rights.* London: The North-South Institute.

Khan, H. (1988). Women and community development in Bangladesh. In M. F. Levy

Each in her own way: Five women leaders of the developing world (pp. 31-59). Boulder, CO: Lynne Riener Publishers.

MacIsaac, N., & Wahid, A. N. M. (1993). The Grameen Bank: Its institutional lessons for rural financing. In A. N. M. Wahid (Ed.), *The Grameen Bank. Poverty relief in Bangladesh* (pp. 191-209). Boulder, CO: Westview Press.

Mayoux, L. (1995). Beyond naiveté: Women, gender inequality and participatory development. *Development and Change, 26*, 235-258.

Midgley, J. (1996). Involving social work in economic development. *International Social Work, 39*, 13-25.

Millar, J., & Glendinning, C. (1989). Survey article: Gender and poverty. *Social Policy, 18*, 363-381.

Miller, D. C. (1990). *Women and social welfare: A feminist analysis.* New York: Praetor.

Missionaries of micro-credit. (1996, January/February). *Canadian Banker, 103*(1), 30.

Mizan, A. N. (1993). Women's decision-making power in rural Bangladesh: A study of the Grameen Bank. In A.N.M. Wahid (Ed.), *The Grameen Bank. Poverty relief in Bangladesh* (pp. 127-153). Boulder, CO: Westview Press.

Mondal, W.I., & Tune, R.A. (1993). Replicating the Grameen Bank in North America: The Good Faith experience. In A. N. M. Wahid (Ed.), *The Grameen Bank. Poverty relief in Bangladesh* (pp. 223-234). Boulder, CO: Westview Press.

Neff, G. (1996, October). Microcredit, microresults. *Left Business Observer, 74*, 5-7.

Novogratz, J. (1992). *Hopeful change. The potential of micro-enterprise programs as a community revitalization intervention.* New York: The Rockefeller Foundation.

Papa, M. J., Auwal, M.A., & Singhal, A. (1995). Dialectic of control and emancipation in organizing for social change. A multitheoretic study of the Grameen Bank in Bangladesh. *Communications Theory, 5*(3), 189-223.

Peterson, V. S., & Runyan, A. S. (1993). *Global gender issues.* Boulder, CO: Westview Press.

Raheim, S. (1996). Micro-enterprise as an approach for promoting economic development in social work: Lessons from the self-employment investment demonstration. *International Social Work, 39*, 69-82.

Raheim, S. (1997). Problems and prospects of self-employment as an economic independence option for welfare clients. *Social Work, 42* (1), 44-55.

Raheim, S., & Bolden, J. (1995). Economic empowerment of low-income women through self-employment programs. *Affilia, 10* (2), 138-154.

Rahman, A. (1993). The general replicability of the Grameen Bank model. In A. N. M. Wahid (Ed.), *The Grameen Bank. Poverty relief in Bangladesh* (pp. 209-221). Boulder, CO: Westview Press.

Rahman, A., & Islam, M.M. (1993). The general performance of the Grameen Bank. In A.N.M. Wahid (Ed.), *The Grameen Bank. Poverty relief in Bangladesh* (pp. 49-69). Boulder, CO: Westview Press.

Rosenthal, M. G. (1994). Single mothers in Sweden: Work and welfare in the welfare state. *Social Work, 39*(3), 270-279.

Schuler, S.R. & Hashemi, S.M. (1995). Family planning outreach and credit programs in rural Bangladesh. *Human Organization, 54* (4), 455-461.

Segal, E. A. (1989). Welfare reform: Help for poor women and children? *Affilia, 4*(3), 42-50.

Sen, G., & Grown, S. (1987). *Development, crisis and alternative visions.* New York: Monthly Review Press.

Severens, C. Alexander and A. J. Kays. (1997). 1996 Directory of U.S. Microenterprise Programs. Washington, DC: Self-Employment Learning Program, The Aspen Institute.

Shams, M.K. (1992). *Designing effective credit delivery system for the poor. The Grameen Bank experience.* Dhaka: Grameen Bank.

Shehabuddin, R. (1992). *The impact of Grameen Bank in Bangladesh. Empowering rural women.* Dhaka: Grameen Bank.

Tinker, I. (1989). Credit for poor women: Necessary, but not always sufficient for change. *Marga, 10*(2), 31-49.

Tinker, I. (1990). *Persistent inequalities.* New York: Oxford University Press.

United Nations. (1991). *The world's women: 1970-1990.* New York: Social Statistics and Indicators, Series K (8).

U.S. General Accounting Office (1993). *Welfare to work: JOBS participation rate data unreliable for assessing states' performance.* Washington, DC: U.S. Government Printing Office.

Van der Wees, C., & Romijn, H. (1995). Entrepreneurship and small- and micro-enterprise development for women: A problem in search of answers, a policy in search of programs. In L. Dignard & J. Havet *Women in micro- and small-scale enterprise development* (pp. 41-85). Boulder, CO: Westview Press.

Wahid, A. N. M. (1993). (Ed.). *The Grameen Bank. Poverty relief in Bangladesh.* Boulder, CO: Westview Press.

Wahid, A. N. M. (1994). The Grameen Bank and poverty alleviation in Bangladesh: Theory, evidence and limitations. *The American Journal of Economics and Sociology, 53*(1), 1-15.

Young, K. (1993). *Planning development with women. Making a world of difference.* New York: St. Martin's Press.

Yunus, M. (1982). *Grameen Bank in Bangladesh. A poverty focused rural development programme.* Dhaka: Grameen Bank.

Yunus, M. (1987). *Credit for self-employment: A fundamental human right.* Dhaka: Grameen Bank.

Yunus, M. (1994a). *Grameen Bank. Does the capitalist system have to be the handmaiden of the rich?* Dhaka: Grameen Bank.

Yunus, M. (1994b). *Credit is a human right.* Dhaka: Grameen Bank.

Community
Economic Development Organizations
in Montreal

Jean-Marc Fontan, PhD
Eric Shragge, PhD

SUMMARY. This chapter explores the dilemmas facing CED intermediary organizations as vehicles for progressive social change
through an analysis of an urban Canadian model from Québec called
corporations de développement économique communautaire (CDEC).
CDECs are democratically controlled, not-for-profit, local development organizations that oversee and support CED efforts on three
main levels: (1) job skills development and "employability" services; (2) business development; and (3) development of innovative
partnerships among diverse groups to plan and coordinate CED
strategies in their communities. These practices are analyzed and issues inherent to them are presented using specific contributions from
CED literature. This analysis shows that within such organizations,
contradictory practices and directions co-exist due to pressures exerted simultaneously by market, state, and community forces. *[Article
copies available for a fee from The Haworth Document Delivery Service:
1-800-342-9678. E-mail address: getinfo@haworthpressinc.com]*

INTRODUCTION

During the past decade, Community Economic Development (CED)
projects and organizations have taken root in communities across Québec

---

Jean-Marc Fontan is Professor of Sociology at Université du Québec à Montréal.
Eric Shragge is Associate Professor in the School of Social Work, McGill
University, Montreal.

[Haworth co-indexing entry note]: "Community Economic Development Organizations in Montreal."
Fontan, Jean-Marc, and Eric Shragge. Co-published simultaneously in *Journal of Community Practice* (The
Haworth Press, Inc.) Vol. 5, No. 1/2, 1998, pp. 125-136; and: *Community Economic Development and Social
Work* (ed: Margaret S. Sherraden, and William A. Ninacs) The Haworth Press, Inc., 1998, pp. 125-136.
Single or multiple copies of this article are available for a fee from The Haworth Document Delivery Service
[1-800-342-9678, 9:00 a.m. - 5:00 p.m. (EST). E-mail address: getinfo@haworthpressinc.com].

125

(Favreau, 1989; Favreau and Ninacs, 1994). This paper examines CED organizations in Montreal called Corporations de développement économique communautaire (CDEC). In this paper, we write about two aspects of the CDECs. We present an overview of their development and practices, and examine specific innovations that they have implemented. Next, we review some differences in CED practice orientation. From this literature, we ask if and how the CDECs contribute to progressive social change. Finally, we will argue that the CDECs exist in a contradictory world shaped, on the one hand, by community and trade union agendas, and on the other hand by the pressures of the neo-liberal state and the market.

THE CDECS

There are seven CDECs[1] in Montreal whose mandate is to intervene and to service one administrative district of the city.[2] The first three began in the late 1980s in older industrial neighborhoods facing urban decay, economic decline, and high levels of unemployment linked to the disappearance of traditional industrial jobs. In the mid-1980s, community activists argued that neither the government nor the private sector appeared able to find ways to address these issues effectively. Therefore, they began new initiatives to develop the local economy and create jobs. Community organizations expanded their activities, and with new partners such as representatives of labor, business, and local government institutions, such as health clinics, put in place CED initiatives in several old industrial communities (Fontan, 1993; Fontan and Shragge, 1997; Gareau, 1990). These new partnerships explored community-based responses to the crisis. Federal and provincial government levels funded these initiatives on a short term basis. The first three CED projects received municipal funding in addition, to formalize the CED structures and to extend the CDEC approach to other parts of Montreal.

The first four CDECs were created through a process of local organizing, while the later ones were initiated by the government, but with structures and processes to give control to the local community. By 1990, an agreement was reached by the municipal, provincial, and federal governments to fund these initiatives and enlarge their number. Currently, the CDEC's budgets range from approximately $500,000 (Can) to $2,000,000 (Can), with an average around $600,000 (Can). Their funding is controlled by a committee chaired by a representative of the City of Montreal, and includes representatives of the provincial and federal levels of government. Each level of government contributes money linked to a specific program that it expects to be carried out locally.

In 1990 the different levels of government agreed on three objectives for the CDECs: (1) to encourage training and integration of the local population into the labor market—"employability services"; (2) to support businesses and entrepreneurs in their development projects to create or maintain jobs; and (3) to develop a partnership between community organizations, businesses, unions, and institutions as the most important way to achieve goals 1 and 2 (Shragge, 1992). In this section we describe the practice of the CDECs. Because we discuss seven different organizations, we present some general directions of practice and the overall impact, as well as examples from different CDECs to illustrate the type of programs that have been undertaken. We examine the accomplishments and the problems in each of these three areas.

Employability Services

These services are intended to develop individual capacities of different categories of unemployed workers so they can enter and remain in the labor market. The services include: information and referral to other programs, workshops on different aspects of employment, and training and educational programs. The individualized services include: help with job searches for self-referred individuals, including the use of a job bank and preparation of personal resumés. One innovative practice is an apprentice-type program for highly trained immigrants to provide them with their first work experiences in Canada.[3] In addition, the CDEC administers government funds to community organizations that establish job training programs. CDECs provide training grants to community organizations to create local businesses with socially oriented services or ecologically oriented businesses. For example, these grants have supported a loan circle program for women developing micro-enterprises, and an anti-poverty group that promoted a furniture and clothing recycling business. One of the strengths of these programs is that they cut across bureaucratic boundaries usually imposed by government, and bring programs to individuals and groups at the local level.

The CDECs' employability programs have produced, on a small scale, better results than those administered by business, school boards and government agencies (Leduc, 1994), at least partly because they have been able to bring together business, labor, and the community to examine local labor market needs and training capacities. Flexibility and innovation are central elements in their success. The lack of decent jobs is a limit that these programs cannot overcome by themselves.

Business Development

The CDECs are directly involved in business development in their respective districts. Most of this practice supports small-scale capitalist initiatives. Examples of their practices include providing advice to individual enterprises such as the development of business plans, consulting management, evaluating the health of businesses, finding sources of financial support–particularly from government, and building links among existing businesses. Activities such as courses, referral to business school students and professors, and individual sessions are the forms these activities take. The results have been the creation of some new businesses, mutual aid, and exchanges. The CDECs have developed loan funds in conjunction with a large trade union fund to stimulate local innovative and high-tech industries. In addition to job creation, CDECs established an efficient interface between government agencies and businesses. This has improved the climate of confidence and facilitated the identification of problems and economic needs at the local level (Fontan, 1988,1990).

CDECs developed other innovative and experimental forms of entrepreneurship such as production cooperatives and businesses that specialize in job training. Job training businesses are one strategy to counter the very high levels of youth unemployment (Bordeleau and Valadou, 1995; Fontan and Shragge, 1994). These have played a dual role of providing innovative community services or socially useful products and doing this by employing trainees. Another innovation is to link social and economic development and/or the incorporation of ecological principles into business. Examples include the development of industries specializing in recycling of glass and/or plastic. CDECs have supported local loan funds and loan circles so that they in turn can encourage a range of small-scale local initiatives. These initiatives then support micro-enterprises for groups usually excluded from the labor market (Merrill, 1997; Mendell and Evoy, 1997).

CDECs have contributed to local economic planning. This includes consulting with the local community and presenting policy proposals to the city. These approaches maximize employment options and/or promote social needs such as non-profit housing. With these approaches, the CDECs have been able to mobilize sectors of the local community and promote socially useful options. The CDEC's new voice in the planning process represents "community interests," which challenges the traditional profit only limits of the market. The following are two examples of how CDECs have influenced the direction of community and market economic development. One CDEC has launched a process in which a large tract of land formerly used in the railway industry will be reconverted into an industrial park for high-tech environmental industry. There will be a training component so that unemployed residents will get jobs and a community board will control land use through a land trust (Shragge and Fontan, 1997). Another CDEC led a community coalition opposing McGill University's decision to locate a dormitory in an old industrial building. A compromise was reached so that local employment was guaranteed in the dormitory, and McGill invested $500,000 (Can) in a social housing fund. In addition, it provided academic resources to community organizations over a five year period (Fontan, 1993a). Both of these examples demonstrate that the CDECs have been able to play a leadership role in shaping local economies, therefore, democratizing economic processes.

Local Partnerships

The third function of the CDECs is to build local partnerships among representatives of business, labor, community organizations and institutions (Panet-Raymond, 1992). Each group on the board of directors of the CDEC participates in and builds these partnerships. Each group uses electoral colleges to select its representatives to the board of directors. Employees are also represented. In addition, CDECs have members from the general public with the average of 150 per CDEC. The numbers are relatively small—the largest, Regroupment Pour la Rélance Economique et Sociale du Sud-Ouest (RESO) has 250 members but only events like annual meetings bring out the highest attendance (Leduc, 1994). CDECs define the local community as both a clientele and as a membership, and have had only limited success in mobilizing large numbers. The CDECs do bring together diverse local interests, but one would not describe them as a mass base organization with wide participation from the grassroots levels. Rather, they represent and discuss interests in an attempt to create consensus on the needs and priorities for local economic development in the context of the state-funded programs.

The results of these partnerships have been different depending on the CDEC. In some districts, the CDECs have become a new voice unifying economic actors, and collaborating to shape the local economic agenda. This has implied decentralization of economic decision-making and increased local control over specific types and conditions of investment decisions. Thus a few of the CDECs have built a local power base and have been effective in influencing local development (Fontan, 1993a). In other districts, conflicts emerged between various interest groups, and slowed or weakened the potential decentralization of power because these groups have been unable to articulate a clear program to take them beyond the specific government program that they administer. The following discussion of the literature is a way to examine the potential of the CDECs as organizations for social change.

PERSPECTIVES ON CED

The central question for us in this paper is whether or not the CDECs are a vehicle for progressive social change, and if so, how is this expressed in practice. What types of practices lead to community empowerment? Are there new forms of production existing that link social and economic development? Is it possible to facilitate democratic decision making on economic issues at the local level? Or are the CDECs only an administrative arm of government putting in place programs that might be innovative but do not lead to collective action? We have selected some of the literature to clarify the different approaches to CED practice, and then in our analysis we discuss the CDECs relative to some of the debates we have found in the literature.

In his review of the international literature on CED, Fontan (1993b) contrasts two perspectives–liberal and progressive. The liberal approach gives business development first priority while the progressive approach defines community empowerment as CED's major goal. He states:

> . . . liberal local initiatives are aimed solely at repairing the economic fiber of the private sector in order to create jobs. . . . In contrast, progressive initiatives invest the economy with social concerns, in order to weave a socio-economic fabric that takes social objectives into account with a view to creating new interdependencies and an economic democracy that fosters greater participation and control on the part of the community in the planning and development of their locality. (p. 8-9)

The liberal approach assumes that through private economic investment, problems like unemployment will be remedied. Some of the characteristics associated with the progressive approach include: the linking of social and economic objectives, according a priority to nontraditional economic forms (cooperatives, community businesses, nonprofit organizations), encouraging local control and/or ownership of resources, and creating organizations to reach these goals that are representative of and accountable to the local community.

Rubin and Rubin (1992) argue that progressive CED practice has two goals: to create more good quality jobs for poor people and to provide workers with more control over the workplace. They propose three approaches to achieve these goals: (1) advocacy that relies on protest and lobbying for economic changes that can benefit low-income communities, (2) quasi-capitalist approaches that use "the tools of capitalism to promote the development of new firms and to help community members learn the skills needed for the modern workplace" (p. 417), (3) alternative development approaches that encourage people to withdraw from the conventional market place and set up alternative forms of economic development and exchange.

The above perspectives clarify the potential and vision for practice, but the realities of negotiating a market economy and communicating with the state create tensions and contradictions. Stoecker (1995) describes these tensions in his critical discussion of CED practice in American community development corporations. They are "caught between worlds." They " . . . manage capital, like capitalists, but don't invest it for a profit. They manage projects, but within the constraints set by their funders. They try to be community oriented while their purse strings are held by outsiders" (p. 4). This description echoes the practices and orientations of the CDECs, and simultaneously allows some space for progressive practice and vision. We argue that within these organizations, contradictory practices and directions co-exist, and this complexity is the core of our analysis.

We selected these three contributions from the literature because they clarify some of the issues that face the CDECs. From Fontan (1993b) we see that emphasizing economic development alone is insufficient for progressive practice. Rubin and Rubin (1992) point out that change-oriented goals require specific strategies and practices and they have proposed three of them. Stoecker (1995) in our view raises the key element in the debate, the underlying tensions in which CED operates. This implies the existence of contradictory values and directions within the same organization and practices. We see these tensions as a useful way to understand the practices of organizations like CDECs.

ANALYSIS

The CDECs are pulled in several directions simultaneously. The levels of government that fund the organizations and the business community promote the view that traditional entrepreneurship is primarily a means of stimulating local development through private sector investment. The community sector often allies with the trade unions that have promoted innovative and collective approaches to economic development. Their

CED agenda stems from a tradition of struggling to keep social and economic rights, increasing the democratization of economic processes as well as trying to improve the material conditions of the poor and unemployed.

Depending on one's tradition, CED can be both a vehicle for social change and/or capitalist development. The failure of the traditional means of economic development and state program cutbacks create a situation in which government views the community sector and CED as a relatively low-cost alternative to the traditional forms of state intervention. The CDECs have responded to these contradictory pressures by using government programs described above and promoting innovative activities. Given the inherent tensions it has not been a simple process.

The culture and expectations of the state and community are different. Success of the various government programs administered through the CDECs is defined by quantifiable outcomes, such as the number of clients seen or jobs created. This insistence on defining accountability through quantifiable measures conflicts with a process orientation of the community that does not define results only on the basis of numbers. One example of this difference is the use of the concept of empowerment. For government, empowerment implies individual change, specifically the individual gaining skills and subsequently entering the labor market. The quantitative approach of government implies an individualized service approach in both training and business development. It translates the consequences of global economic change into issues of individual deficit and business planning.

For the community, empowerment implies effective participation and control of economic and social processes, as well as participation in allocating resources and using programs at the local level (Friedman, 1992). The community sector created approaches that assume collective management and build local networks of solidarity and support, referred to as a social economy (Lipietz, 1989; Levesque, Joyal and Chouinard, 1989). These competing visions, of local development and community economic development, to use Fontan's concepts, co-exist. This tension will exist as long as both visions are present in the process. One of the key difficulties is to develop an alternative vision that can be translated into practice.

Returning to Rubin and Rubin (1992), CDECs combine all three forms of practice. By defending their programs and services CDECs advocate for changes to low-income communities, and mobilize local organizations to promote specific interests like job creation. CDECs show quasi-capitalist development by supporting a variety of business ventures from micro-enterprises to traditional businesses. CDECs exhibit alternative approaches by supporting cooperatives that promote social development through economic activities. In many of these activities, groups marginalized by the rapid changes in a global economy can participate in these new forms of economic development. However, because the CDECs administer pre-defined government programs, they lean toward traditional means to achieve their goal.

Given the contradictions in which CDECs operate, what have they achieved, what is their impact, particularly their potential to promote and support social change? The most difficult problem is the CDECs' inability to resolve the basic issues of poverty and unemployment. These basic questions include the division of wealth and macro-economic and social policy. Clearly, this wider context has generated greater unemployment, increased poverty, and divided the new jobs between the some that pay decently and the rest that provide part time, low wage work. Further, government policy has done little to redress these problems. Its economic policies have worsened the problems by limiting state spending and ignoring unemployment. The CDECs can do little about the wider policies except push with others for change.

One major achievement of the CDECs is their innovative forms of socio-economic development. Training businesses link social production with job skills development, loan circles forge solidarity, and ecological cooperatives are a new model for sustainable development. These innovations have produced a few jobs, and at the same time, have put in place what can be described as social-economic development. These are community businesses, not for private profit, that enhance the social functioning of the community. In addition, many of these projects allow groups usually excluded from the mainstream economy to find a productive place in a solidaristic environment. These innovations are important because they contribute to the social economy and allow collective control over the form of production.

Perhaps the most important achievement of the CDECs is their contribution to the democratization of economic processes at the local level. In contrast to a concept of individualized empowerment discussed above, the CDECs promote a collective approach. This argues for effective participation of the community through managing local but decentralized programs. This collective approach has resulted in the local control of training budgets and the capacity to use these funds with innovation. In addition, the CDECs influence local economic development. The private sector, which usually shapes this process in conjunction with the state, has had to face a wider process in its economic decision-making. The community sector and the trade unions have been able to use the CDECs to raise demands for jobs and social concerns in the developmental process.

The question we raise is how far can this process go; what are the limits of a state-funded organization? The tensions that Stoecker discusses are central in understanding both the potential and the limits of the CDECs. The local community as represented in the CDECs seems to be a gathering place where various interests, using reciprocity and compromise, can find ways to solve social problems. The CDECs have maneuvered within the pre-defined government programs to promote innovation and give those with a progressive vision a forum for experimenting. However, to move ahead, CDECs must address two remaining issues. The first is their inability to mobilize large numbers of people at the local level and build a common agenda. Second, the gains at the local level are always limited and the CDECs have done little to challenge the government on the wider social and policy issues that have a profound impact on local development. CDECs have made some progressive gains locally, but at the same time, the source of the problem is the economic system itself and the politics that support it. Unless these are challenged, then the CDECs will broker only small gains and remain a minor player in the global economic processes that helped destroy, eliminate, or remove jobs from their community.

NOTES

1. There are two sources for the following information. The first source is references used throughout the text. The second source of information is the observations of both authors who have been involved in these organizations for many years.

2. The City of Montreal is divided into administrative districts called arrondisements. There is one CDEC for each except in the downtown core.

3. These examples are taken from the CDEC Côtes-des Neiges/Notre-Dame de Grâces, which works in an ethnically diverse community. It has little large-scale manufacturing, but universities and hospitals provide some employment.

REFERENCES

Bordeleau, D., and Valadou, C. (1995). *Agir pour l'insertion: initiatives d'insertion par l'économique au Québec.* Montreal: Institut de formation en développement économique communautaire (IFDEC).

Favreau, L. (1989). *Mouvement populaire et intervention communautaire de 1960 à nos jours, continuités et ruptures.* Montréal: Centre de formation populaire et les éditions du Fleuve.

Favreau, L., and Ninacs, W. A. (1994). "The Innovative Profile of Community Economic Development in Quebec" in Galaway, B. and Hudson, J. (Eds) *Community Economic Development: Perspectives on Research and Policy*, Toronto: Thompson Educational Publishing, pp. 153-165.

Fontan, J-M. (1988). "Dévelopment économique communautaire à Montréal." *Possibles*, Vol. 12, No. 2, pp. 183-200.

Fontan, J-M. (1990). "Les corporations de développement économique communautaire: une des avenues du mouvement social dans l'économique" *Coopératives et dévelopment*, Vol. 21, no. 2. pp. 32-41.

Fontan, J-M. (1993a). "Pointe St. Charles: Building a Community Voice" in Shragge, E. (editor) *Community Economic Development: In Search of Empowerment*. Montreal: Black Rose Books, pp. 76-92.

Fontan, J-M, (1993b). *A Critical Review of Canadian, American, and European Community Economic Development Literature*. Vancouver: Centre for Community Enterprise.

Fontan, J-M. and Shragge, E. (1994). "Employability Approaches in CED Practice: Case Studies and Issues" in Gallaway, B. and Hudson, J. (editors) *Community Economic Development: Canadian Research and Policy Perspectives*, Toronto: Thompson Educational Publishing, pp. 144-152.

Friedman, J. (1992). *Empowerment: The Politics of Alternative Development*. Cambridge (MA) and Oxford: Blackwell.

Gareau, J-M. (1990). *Le programme économique de Pointe Saint-Charles, la percée du dévelopment économique communautaire dans le Sud-ouest de Montréal*. Montréal: IFDEC.

Leduc, M. (1994). *Evaluation des corporations de développement économique communautaire: rapport déposé au Comité d'harmonisation de Montréal*. Montréal: IFDEC.

Levesque, B., Joyal, A., and Chouinard, O. (1989). *L'autre économie: une économie alternative?* Sillery: Presses de l'Université du Québec.

Lipietz, A. (1989). *Choisir l'audace: une alternative pour le XXIe siècle*. Paris: Éditions la découverte.

Mendell, M. and Evoy, L. (1997). "Democratizing Capital: Alternative Investment Strategies" in Shragge, E. (editor) *Community Economic Development: In Search of Empowerment and Alternatives* (2nd ed). Montreal: Black Rose Books, pp. 110-129.

Merrill, S. (1997). "Loan Circles: The Montreal Experience" in Shragge, E. (editor) *Community Economic Development: In Search of Empowerment and Alternatives* (2nd ed). Montreal: Black Rose Books, pp. 130-146.

Panet-Raymond, J. (1992). "Partnership: Myth or Reality?" *Community Development Journal*, Vol. 27, No. 2, April, pp. 156-165.

Rubin, H. J. and Rubin, I. S. (1992). *Community Organizing and Developing* (2nd ed). New York: Macmillan.

Shragge, E. and Fontan, J-M. (1997). "CED in Montreal: Community versus State Control" in Shragge, E. (editor) *Community Economic Development: In*

Search of Empowerment and Alternatives (2nd ed). Montreal: Black Rose Books, pp. 87-109.

Shragge E. (1992). "Community Economic Development in Montreal: Some Political Questions," *City Magazine*, Vol. 13, No.1, Winter 91/92 pp. 30-35.

Stoecker, R. (1995). *Empowering Development: Toward a Different CDC* from web site www. nhi.org/ online/ issues/ 87/cdcmodel.html

Low-Income Homeownership Policy as a Community Development Strategy

Edward Scanlon, MSW

SUMMARY. Homeownership for the poor increasingly is on the political agenda in the United States. This is due largely to the assumptions made by policy makers and citizens about the benefits of homeownership. Despite this emphasis in recent administrations, little theoretical literature has been developed that specifies the impact of homeownership on community development. This essay reviews relevant theoretical and empirical literature and suggests that homeownership affects communities through the promotion of increased wealth accumulation, improved property upkeep, decreased residential mobility, and increased community participation. This article addresses the special needs of poor communities and households, and the implications for low-income housing policy. Overall it is suggested that community economic development and low-income homeownership be pursued in tandem. *[Article copies available for a fee from The Haworth Document Delivery Service: 1-800-342-9678. E-mail address: getinfo@haworthpressinc.com]*

A primary strategy of community economic development has been the production of low- and moderate-income housing. Housing development has also been prompted by a recognition of both the beneficial effects of housing on the overall economy of the community and positive impacts

Edward Scanlon is a doctoral student at the George Warren Brown School of Social Work, and Research Associate at the Center for Social Development, Washington University in St. Louis, One Brookings Drive, Campus Box 1196, St. Louis, MO 63130 (E-mail: etscanlo@artsci.wustl.edu).

[Haworth co-indexing entry note]: "Low-Income Homeownership Policy as a Community Development Strategy." Scanlon, Edward. Co-published simultaneously in *Journal of Community Practice* (The Haworth Press, Inc.) Vol. 5, No. 1/2, 1998, pp. 137-154; and: *Community Economic Development and Social Work* (ed: Margaret S. Sherraden, and William A. Ninacs) The Haworth Press, Inc., 1998, pp. 137-154. Single or multiple copies of this article are available for a fee from The Haworth Document Delivery Service [1-800-342-9678, 9:00 a.m. - 5:00 p.m. (EST). E-mail address: getinfo@haworthpressinc.com].

137

for households (Hays, 1995). The serious shortage of adequate low-income housing has made such development paramount to policy makers and community developers (Stone, 1993).

Typically, development efforts have focused on the production or rehabilitation of rental housing. Community development corporations (CDCs) and non-profit housing agencies have become involved in the development and management of rental properties, and federal policy has provided tax credits for developers of low-income rental properties. Increasingly, CDCs and non-profits are buying, renovating, developing and managing such properties as anchors for distressed urban areas (Salsich, 1993).

While such strategies are important in expanding the gravely limited low-income housing stock, some policy analysts criticize concentrating initiatives on rental properties (Sherraden, 1991; Johnson and Sherraden, 1992). A growing body of work is focusing on the social and economic outcomes that result from different forms of housing tenure. In these studies, it is becoming clearer that homeownership generates beneficial outcomes for households and communities. Suggested outcomes include, at the household level, enhanced psychological functioning (Rohe and Stegman, 1994a; Green and White, 1994), increased social participation (Rohe and Stegman, 1994b), greater life satisfaction (Rohe and Stegman, 1994a), and increased wealth and savings (Oliver and Shapiro, 1995). At the level of community, enhanced property values, improved neighborhood stability and increased neighborhood participation can result from homeownership (Galster, 1987; Rohe and Stewart, 1996).

The extent to which homeownership promotes community and household well-being is not understood clearly, although empirical evidence for such effects is growing. Theoretical mechanisms that explain homeownership effects are also not well specified. Nonetheless, homeownership for the poor is increasingly on the political agenda, and this paper begins with an examination of this policy trend. This paper then explores the theoretical literature and offers four empirical propositions regarding the community development effects of homeownership. Recommendations are made for further research, policy and community development. Overall, community revitalization strategies and homeownership programs must develop simultaneously to make either work effectively.

A DESCRIPTION OF LOW-INCOME HOMEOWNERSHIP PROGRAMS

In recent years, both the Bush and Clinton administrations have expressed concern about stagnating homeownership rates, and considered homeownership as a potential solution for the crisis in public and low-income housing (DeParle, 1991; US Department of Housing and Urban Development, 1995; Hays, 1995). Many community groups advocate low-income homeownership programs and call for more empirical investigation of homeownership impacts (Rohe and Stegman, 1994a; Stegman, 1993). These programs are seen as an alternative to public housing and low-income rental subsidies, and can be understood as an alternative to the policy of low-income housing provided by the government. This trend of privatization has been followed by a number of European governments as well as the United States in a variety of social, health, and welfare programs.

Through the mechanisms of federal banking policy and the tax system, the United States government has promoted homeownership for middle and upper income Americans since the New Deal era (Hays, 1995). Between the late 1940s and 1980, homeownership increased dramatically, moving from 44% to 65.5% (Dreier and Atlas, 1992). These rates are not distributed uniformly across race and class, however, as the poor and minorities are far less likely to own than are affluent and white heads of household (Oliver and Shapiro, 1995). After 1980, homeownership rates leveled off at about 66%, and have remained there. For some groups, such as minorities, the poor and younger people, homeownership rates have actually declined since 1980 (US Department of Housing and Urban Development, 1996).

The federal government has made minor efforts to encourage home-ownership among the poor, but typically these have been short-lived and inadequate for making significant differences in overall homeownership rates among this population. The Section 235 program, for example, provided subsidies to low-income home buyers which reduced their mortgage loan interest rate to below market values. The program was marked by scandal, however, and a default rate of 20% of the loans insured between 1968 and 1973. The program was eliminated in the Nixon moratorium on government housing programs in the early 1970s (Hays, 1995; Silver, McDonald and Ortiz, 1985).

In 1990, Jack Kemp, the Bush administration's Secretary of Housing and Urban Development, again took up the gauntlet of home ownership for the poor. Kemp, a former congressman from Buffalo, New York, had a strong ideological attachment to an entrepreneurial approach to social welfare, and wanted to create urban and housing policies that would encourage the poor to participate in the same economic structures as middle and upper income citizens. Kemp supported legislation that would allow such participation, such as homeownership programs, enterprise zones, and business development for the poor. A centerpiece of his housing policy was the Home Ownership for People Everywhere (HOPE) program. Kemp wanted a new "conservative war on poverty," and despite the opposition of many in the Bush administration, was able to convince a Democratic congress to pass his HOPE program (DeParle, 1991).

The HOPE program was structured to provide benefits in a manner that is increasingly common among such programs. These low-income home-ownership programs typically subsidize housing prices directly or through reductions of interest rates to below market levels. They frequently provide assistance with closing costs and points, or allow these to be financed in the loan. Often, these programs will reduce or subsidize the down-payment and provide subsidies for incidental legal fees or other expenses. Finally, they often provide money for programs to prepare potential buyers financially for homeownership and to learn necessary skills such as home repair (US Department of Housing and Urban Development, 1992).

The Clinton administration has made homeownership the centerpiece of its housing policy as well. In 1995, President Clinton announced his administration's National Homeownership Strategy, a series of 100 recommendations to increase national homeownership rates to an all time high of 67.5% within five years. The strategy uses existing institutions and community organizations to expand information and access to credit as well as strategies to lessen down-payment and closing costs. The National Homeownership Strategy was produced by HUD in partnership with private groups such as the American Bankers Association and Fannie Mae ("Clinton Pushes," 1995).

These programs have been justified with many of the arguments that have historically been made for homeownership. These claims–that home-owning brings psychological benefits, raises self-esteem, stabilizes finances, and encourages community development, home improvement, and neighborhood involvement–are commonly made by citizens, social scientists and policy elites. In the following section, this paper reviews the theoretical literature regarding the effects of homeownership at the community level.

THEORETICAL MODELS OF THE EFFECTS OF HOMEOWNERSHIP

Limited theoretical literature exists regarding the effects of homeownership. The investment return theory of homeownership is based on the idea that homeownership promotes positive outcomes for homeowners because of the increasing economic equity that is earned. In this view, it is economically logical for homeowners to act in ways that will protect their economic investment in a home. Thus homeownership engenders behaviors such as community involvement and home improvement because they make economic sense.

Investment Return Theory advocates point to the difference in household assets held by homeowners and renters, noting that homeowner median net wealth in the United States is $78,400 while for renters it is $2,300. For minority and low-income households, home equity makes up more than 50% of accumulated household wealth. For these authors, the wealth accumulation associated with homeownership is proof that it is a beneficial form of housing tenure. However, these authors also argue that the economic investment of homeowning results in improved property maintenance and hence overall valuation of the housing stock. Thus, homeowners make better neighbors because they have an economic incentive to be better neighbors (Butler, 1985; Linneman and Megbolugbe, 1992; US Department of Housing and Urban Development, 1995).

Farmer and Barrell (1981) argue that home buying is lucrative financially in a way that most investments are not, because few other investments provide the level of stable returns earned in housing purchases. This benefit, as Merrett (1982) argues, leads to significant changes in behavior, thoughts and attitudes. Yates (1982) echoes Merrett, claiming:

> Home-owners tend to be more prepared to pay for the upkeep and maintenance of their properties, since they have a financial interest in maintaining or increasing a home's capital value; tenants do not. The condition of the housing stock is therefore more likely to be maintained with owner occupation than with renting. (p. 218)

Stuart Butler (1985) has argued that private home ownership, because it provides owners with a financial stake in their communities, enhances community involvement. Butler argues, in a 1985 book about privatization, that the poor are encouraged to improve their communities because of the financial gains that flow from enhanced property values.

Asset theory, proposed by Michael Sherraden (1991), provides an alternative concept of the effects of homeownership that has both economic and psychological elements. While his theory is not specific to housing assets, and in fact focuses on holding a range of asset types, it can easily be extended to homeowning. In a critique of social welfare policy based on income maintenance, Sherraden asserts the superiority of asset based welfare as a means of decreasing poverty and of generating socially desirable behavior. Assets are the stock of wealth in a household or other unit (Sherraden, 1991). Sherraden sees asset based policy as important because it sees well-being as a cumulative, dynamic process, resulting from a life time of stored efforts and accrued wealth. Income based policy, conversely, sees well-being as merely a reflection of consumption capacity. Since welfare policy for the poor is based on income maintenance, the poor are shut out of the asset accumulation process and are unable to generate that form of well-being. The poor are then unable to escape poverty, because "few have been able to spend their way out of poverty" (Sherraden, 1991, p. 7). Savings, stored wealth–assets–are necessary for the kinds of cushioning and security needed to exit poverty.

Further, Sherraden theorizes that in addition to providing greater economic security for the poor, having assets also would affect their behavior beneficially. He identifies a set of behaviors that he thinks might result from asset accumulation. These include: (1) greater future orientation, (2) stimulated development of other assets, (3) improved household financial stability, (4) greater focus and specialization, (5) a foundation for risk-taking, (6) increased personal efficacy, (7) increased social influence, (8) increased political participation and (9) enhanced welfare of offspring (Sherraden, 1991).

These behaviors, suggests Sherraden, would result in an approach to the world that would decrease the likelihood of continued poverty, and increase income and asset holding. The policy of asset based welfare would create a virtuous cycle in which asset accumulation and positive social behaviors would be mutually reinforcing. What mechanisms account for these behaviors?

To answer this question, Sherraden introduces the concepts of stakeholding and cognitive schemata. Owning assets gives residents a stake in the system, including them as participants in the social order and offering them some reason to participate in economic and social affairs. The assets, Sherraden reasons, alter the very cognitive schemata of the poor. Experiences of the world interject frameworks that structure one's expectations and understandings of self, world, and future. With current conditions of welfare and poverty, the poor hold perceptions of causality in the world–schemata–that do not promote future orientation or a sense of personal efficacy. Sherraden reasons that assets would alter their cognitive schemata, providing them with mental structures that could incorporate the importance of asset accumulation. Future orientation, risk taking, efficacy, etc., would be behavioral and attitudinal results of a cognitive schemata oriented toward accumulation of assets. Clearly, such changes at the household level have implications for building more stable communities through improved citizenship, property maintenance and greater future orientation.

Peter Saunders (1978; 1990) has also suggested that homeownership benefits the life chances of individuals primarily through asset accumulation. He sees this as especially important in providing security for old age and a cushion against income decreases after retirement. Further, homeowners benefit because they no longer have monthly housing costs, as opposed to elderly tenants, who are still paying rent. Saunders suggests that financial gains can be made by homeowners through property value increases, inflation, tax deductions and their ability to use their own labor to increase the value of their property.

Kemeny (1981) and Doling and Stafford (1989) question this, suggesting that it misunderstands the dynamics of housing for low-income homebuyers. These low-income homebuyers may actually lose money through property devaluation that occurs in deteriorating neighborhoods, or at least may experience lower returns on their investments than upper income home owners. Income shocks and instabilities are more likely to result in evictions and housing repossessions (Meyer, Yeager and Burayidi, 1994). Further, housing repair costs and the generally worse condition of low-cost housing might create financial burdens for poorer homeowners that make home purchase less attractive (Whitehead, 1979; Meyer et al., 1994). This simplistic theory regarding homeowning may not apply equally well to all households. Reviewing these theories suggests four propositions about the relationship between homeownership and community development.

HOMEOWNERSHIP AND COMMUNITY DEVELOPMENT

This reading of the theoretical literature suggests at least four propositions about the relationship between homeownership and community development. These are presented below along with empirical findings regarding each. Homeownership seems to be valued as a community development tool because: (1) it promotes economic development through wealth accumulation, (2) it promotes property maintenance and upkeep, (3) it promotes neighborhood stability through decreased residential turnover and, (4) it promotes increased community participation and neighborhood involvement. What empirical evidence exists for these propositions?

Proposition 1: Homeownership Promotes Community Development Through Increased Household Wealth Accumulation

Community developers want to promote household financial stability; financially stable households are valued for their social influence, tax contributions and community involvement. Empirical literature provides support for the claim that for most households, homeowning promotes financial stabilization. A number of studies have pointed to the financial and economic benefits of homeowning. Page-Adams and Vosler (1997) studied 193 auto-workers, and controlling for income and education, found that homeownership significantly reduced subjects' perceived difficulty of economic strain.

National studies of homeownership equity point to its central role in total wealth among American households. Homeowners have consistently demonstrated greater wealth and equity than renter households. The United States Department of Housing and Urban Development (1995) reports that median net worth for homeowners exceeds $78,400 while for renters it falls below $2,300. This is even more true for minorities, for whom home equity represents almost three-fourths of median net worth of almost $48,300, compared to $500 for renters. Oliver and Shapiro (1995), in a secondary analysis of surveys of 11,257 US households during 1987-1989, found that home equity accounted for 43.3% of white household wealth and 62.5% of black household wealth. Thus homeowners, regardless of race, are likely to have more wealth accrued than are renters.

An additional question is whether homeownership performs well as an investment. General trend data suggest that owner-occupied homes have performed well as long term investments. HUD (1995) found that the median priced home increased in value by a total of 41% between 1960 and 1989, and the lowest priced homes by almost 30% in the same period. Gyourko and Linneman (1993) in a study of housing affordability, examined data from the Annual Housing Survey and found that in the period 1960-1989, homes across the price distribution increased on average. From 1980-1989, however, housing prices decreased, particularly for lower cost homes. This suggests that while overall housing was a good investment, those who purchased in the 1980s and those who purchased lower cost homes may accrue less wealth, or even negative equity.

These data are further complicated by additional studies that suggest that homeownership does not perform equally well in terms of wealth accumulation for minorities and the poor, probably because of neighborhood conditions that decrease housing values. Oliver and Shapiro (1995) analyzed housing value increases for blacks and whites between 1967-1988 and found a $52,000 increase for whites and a $31,000 increase for blacks. The authors concluded that discrimination in real estate markets and racial segregation cost black households in terms of increases in equity. Similarly, Parcel (1982) studied 375 black and 820 white homeowners and found significant differences in housing equity accumulation; this was at least in part due to SMSA differences, again suggesting the role of neighborhood segregation in reducing equity. Long and Caudill (1992) examined racial differences in homeownership and housing wealth in the United States between 1970-1986 and found that blacks were less likely to have accrued housing equity due to lower owner-ship rates and to the lower market values of black owned homes. Neigh-borhood location effects, suggest Long and Caudill, may account for those lower housing values and the resulting decrease of assets.

Doling and Stafford (1989), examining homeownership in Coventry, England, come to similar conclusions and warn of the potential for lower returns and even negative equity for low-income homeowners. According to these authors, neighborhood conditions, repair costs, and income insta-bilities resulting in foreclosure can prevent low-income households from benefiting from homeownership.

Proposition 2: Homeownership Promotes Community Development Through Enhanced Property Maintenance

Community development specialists value concentrated homeowner-ship because it is assumed that increased care of property will result in enhanced property values. The property valuation is important because of the fiscal benefit from increased property taxes. Empirical research by Galster (1983; 1987) confirms that homeowners are more likely than renters or landlords to engage in repair and home maintenance. Others have confirmed this finding (Mayer, 1981). Two studies that utilized direct observation of units found that owner occupied units were 10 to 15% less likely to have structural problems (Jeffers and Dobos, 1984; Kasarda and Janowitz, 1974); Rohe and Stewart (1996) note, however, that they did not look specifically at units in low-income areas. These authors also note that no direct evidence exists that demonstrates a relationship between propor-tion of homeowners in an area and overall level of property upkeep. In other words, research relating owner occupation and upkeep has generally been conducted only at the household level, although effects have been found there consistently.

Proposition 3: Homeownership Promotes Community Development Through Residential Stabilization Accomplished by Decreased Household Tenure Mobility

A number of empirical studies contend that homeownership stabilizes neighborhoods. This occurs through decreased turnover or resident mobility, as residents live longer in geographic areas, anchoring the social relationships and commitment to the neighborhood. Studies by Forrest (1987) and Pickvance (1973) suggest that there is empirical evidence that movers tend to be younger, single and renters. Similarly, Rohe and Stewart (1996) found through a longitudinal analysis of census data that homeownership was positively related to less residential mobility and greater property value appreciation. Butler and Kaiser (1971) found through a survey of 1,476 households that renters and central city dwellers were more likely than others to change residence. McHugh (1985) also found in a study of 167 households in two metropolitan areas that homeowning was negatively associated with residential turnover. However, recent research has also indicated that elderly homeowners are three times more likely than young homeowners to stay in crime-ridden, distressed communities, which raises a potential concern about the residential permanence that results from homeowning (Buckhauser, Butrica and Wasylenko, 1995).

Proposition 4: Homeownership Promotes Community Development Through Increased Involvement in Neighborhood Community Associations

Community developers also value neighbors involved in the planning and progress of the area. Because of widespread concern that Americans are underinvolved in civic organizations–the so-called "bowling alone" phenomenon (Putnam, 1995), some have suggested that homeowners are more likely to be active citizens.

Empirical studies of homeownership have focused on civic involvement (in voluntary associations) and neighboring (providing help to neighbors). Rohe and Stegman (1994b) found that low-income homeowners were more likely than renters to be involved civically, but only at neighborhood or block levels. Perkins, Florin, Rich, Wandersman, and Chavis (1990), examining 48 blocks in New York City, found that the proportion of homeowners on a block impacted civic involvement, but only at individual levels. Other studies confirm that home owners are more likely to be involved in civic organizations (Baum and Kingston, 1984; Cox, 1982; Ditkovsky and van Vliet, 1984; Steinberger, 1981), and to be involved in individual and collective political action (Guest and Oropesa, 1986).

Fischer (1982) and Baum and Kingston (1984) analyzed survey results from 50 localities in Northern California and reported that homeowners were more likely to neighbor. Hunter (1975), examining homeowners in Rochester, New York, also found positive correlations between ownership tenure and informal neighboring. However, Saunders (1990), in a study of British towns, found that homeowners were less likely than renters to know their neighbors and were less likely to neighbor. Fischer, Jackson,

Stueve, Gerson, and Jones (1977) found through analyzing a national sample of citizens that, controlling for length of residence, presence of children and home value, owners were no more likely to neighbor than renters. Rossi and Weber (1996), examining evidence from several data sources, found that owners had fewer social ties to neighbors but were more likely to engage in leadership behavior in local community organizations.

DISCUSSION AND RESEARCH IMPLICATIONS

What can we conclude about the effectiveness of homeownership as a development strategy to promote (1) community economic development, (2) enhancement of neighborhood property values through property upkeep, (3) increased neighborhood stability, and (4) greater community participation?

First, the data suggest that homeownership remains a good investment in the United States, particularly for middle and upper income households. Lower income people and minorities may have different experiences with homebuying, however, and caution should be taken in assuming that such investments are always economically beneficial. Neighborhood conditions and racial segregation may overwhelm beneficial economic effects of home purchase. Further, some middle and upper income households who invested at the peak of the housing market may experience a loss of investment as the market corrects itself (Hughes, 1991). Research should examine the conditions under which low-income people and minorities are at risk for loss of investment when purchasing homes and should specify when homeownership does and does not have the potential to stabilize deteriorating neighborhoods.

Second, solid if limited evidence exists for the property enhancement effects of homeownership. Owner occupiers appear to spend more time and money on property maintenance than either renters or landlords, but again, these effects need to be examined more fully in low-income areas. It is also important to note that unexpected repairs and maintenance problems have been correlated with mortgage payment difficulties among low-income homeowners, suggesting that property upkeep is a strain for such households (Meyer, Yeager and Burayidi, 1994).

Third, the research linking homeownership with decreased tenure mobility is strong, and should be examined further, particularly in regard to low income communities. While permanent residence is valuable, and intuitively seems a social good, it may be problematic for the worst neighborhoods. Residential permanence in the worst areas may reflect declining property values that trap homeowners, particularly the elderly, in homes they literally cannot afford to leave. Such citizens may become victims of crime and collapsing physical and social infrastructure.

Fourth, the relationship between homeownership and social and political involvement appears to be fairly strong. Homeowners do appear to be more involved in neighborhood and community organizations, although the exact nature of the civic involvement of owner-occupiers should be clarified. It is less clear that homeowners make better neighbors than do renters, in the sense of interpersonal involvement and helping behaviors. Research in this area should specify the nature of the involvement of homeowners and should clarify whether these effects, and their meanings, are different for low-income homeowners. It is unclear how neighborhood conditions create different outcomes for homeowners and we must be cautious in extrapolating from studies in middle-income communities.

Finally, research designs should further clarify how homeownership, as opposed to high quality rental housing, promotes community development. Current research usually examines direct relationships between homeownership status and dependent variables with no aspect of the design examining indirect effect variables. For example, homeownership effects may be mediated by cognitions (Sherraden, 1991), wealth accumulation (Saunders, 1978; 1990) or social status (Perin, 1977). Further research is needed before any conclusions can be drawn about these processes, and we must admit that the literature to date is largely atheoretical.

POLICY IMPLICATIONS

Considering all of the existing evidence, three policy implications follow from the above analysis.

1. *Federal tax policy that promotes homeownership in middle- and upper-class neighborhoods is generating spatially organized economic inequalities.* Tax policy should be altered to equalize neighborhood, class and racial disparities in homeownership opportunities. If the positive effects of homeownership create life experiences different for tenants than for owners, then homeowning places people on unequal footings in the class structure. The disparities that result from tenure differences appear to decrease the life chances of those who rent. By establishing policies that promote greater likelihood of ownership tenure among the middle- and upper-class citizens in certain neighborhoods, we have created policies which solidify inequality (Oliver and Shapiro, 1995). This occurs in two ways.

First, as homeowners are far more likely to accumulate wealth, tenants are directly pushed lower in the class structure by this wealth accumulation inequity. Homeownership appears to provide substantial economic benefits, and lower income households who are unlikely to put money in other investments are especially disadvantaged by the failure to own. Tenure differences, which correlate with neighborhood locations, are contributing directly through economic mechanisms of wealth accumulation to spatially based class inequality in the United States.

Second, if homeownership increases involvement in neighborhood and community, tenure may be responsible for providing greater opportunities for networks and social capital. This again provides those with neighborhoods with more homeownership with greater social advantages through the sort of upward mobility that occurs through informal networks and relationships.

The implication of this cemented inequality is that social policy must seek ways to address the inequity in homeownership and to increase homeownership in poor and minority neighborhoods. Currently, the mortgage interest tax deduction is a primary mechanism by which the federal government promotes homeownership. In 1994 (the last year for which data is available), the tax expenditure for mortgage interest was $54.8 billion and local property tax deduction expenditures totaled $14.7 billion (US Department of Treasury, 1994). In 1995 that tax deduction was projected to cost the Treasury $83.3 billion. That benefit inordinately aids middle and upper income homeowners (Kemper, 1994); the top .7% of American households received 10.6% of the deduction benefits in 1993. Capping the mortgage interest tax deduction on mortgages worth above $250,000 could provide $7 billion annually by the year 2000 (Kemper); this could be used as a source of funds to promote homeownership among the poor, minorities, and those in distressed communities.

2. Homeownership benefits may be attenuated by overwhelming neighborhood conditions such as crime, poverty, infrastructure deterioration, unemployment and violence. Therefore, promotion of homeownership should be pursued in tandem with community stabilization efforts.

An overview of studies regarding homeownership suggests less positive effects for people in low-income neighborhoods. This occurs because: (1) less equity can accumulate for those living in poor and minority neighborhoods where housing values are lower, or (2) homeownership benefits are reduced through the social and psychological effects of exposure to crowding, crime, poverty, and physical deterioration. Differential homeownership effects by neighborhood is cause for concern, and the reasons should be studied further.

Nevertheless, the fact that homeownership does confer economic and social benefits in poor neighborhoods suggests its potential for buffering some deleterious effects of negative community conditions. Because of this, homeownership in poor areas should continue to be promoted as a development strategy, even as we identify neighborhoods that can and cannot benefit from such intervention. Simultaneously, cities must engage in neighborhood revitalization which recognizes the importance of strong, safe and attractive neighborhoods as the context for which homeownership is most likely to provide benefits.

Such efforts are already underway and should be encouraged. Community Development Corporations, community banks, and credit unions are beginning to focus on homeowning and increasing homeownership rates in distressed areas. Those who focus on increasing access to mortgage credit for the poor through vigorous enforcement of the Community Reinvestment Act are concerned with the distribution of that capital into poor neighborhoods. Simply put, housing policy should be consciously directed to the task of stabilizing distressed communities and community development should focus on promoting owner occupied housing.

To suggest that homeownership can effectively become the centerpiece of low-income housing policy in 1998 would, however, be irresponsible. Homeownership for the poor is not currently an advanced enough policy to replace in whole the development of low-income rental properties in distressed communities. There are many low-income households that will not, or cannot, become homeowners. The Clinton administration's current goal of reaching overall homeownership rates of 67.5% by the year 2000 is a very limited one in terms of the growing need for affordable, high-quality, low-income housing. In the short term, policy makers need to determine the appropriate mix of rental and owner occupation strategies in distressed communities, and make certain that poor communities have equity in housing options. In the long-term, low-income housing policy should be directed toward homeownership.

3. *The income instabilities of poor and working class families suggest potential for loan default due to income fluctuations or sudden financial stresses related to homeowning such as property tax increases or home repair.* Therefore, low-income homeownership programs must be structured to decrease the risk of income shocks in causing loan default.

The sudden nature of disability, illness, unemployment, or unexpected bills increases the likelihood for families with marginal incomes to default on home loans. Policy should be constructed to assist poor people in avoiding default. At least three strategies can reduce the risk. First, housing programs can offer home repair courses and counseling for potential homeowners so that they can repair minor problems at low cost. Second, insurance programs can provide temporary unemployment or disability insurance to meet mortgage payments. Third, back-up savings accounts can be created as a funding source for home repairs or mortgage payments in emergencies. Such accounts can be required to secure loans and monthly deposits can be required along with mortgage payments. This is currently being done successfully by the Justine Peterson Housing and Community Reinvestment Corporation in St. Louis, and a program of matching deposits for the savings accounts is being planned.

CONCLUSION

In sum, evidence suggests that there are positive effects of homeowning on community development due to wealth accumulation, increased care of properties, stabilized tenure, and increased community involvement. However, difficult neighborhood conditions can reduce these positive impacts and household income streams must be sufficient and stable enough to make homeownership feasible and beneficial. Therefore, home-ownership strategies should be pursued in tandem with community revitalization.

Homeownership programs for the poor should be constructed with attention to the circumstances of poor households and low-income neighborhoods. When this occurs, such programs have the potential to help stabilize communities, promote personal well-being and contribute to economic development. Equally important in a period of social policy stagnation and legislative gridlock, such programs fit with the American traditions of home, neighborhood, and civic commitment, resonating positively among Americans who continue to value homeownership as an essential aspect of the American dream.

REFERENCES

Baum, T. & Kingston, P. (1984). Homeownership And Social Attachment. *Sociological Perspectives, 27, 2,* 159-180.

Buckhauser, R., Butrica, B. & Wasylenko, M. (1995). Mobility Patterns Of Older Homeowners: Are Older Homeowners Trapped In Distressed Neighborhoods? *Research on Aging, 17, 4,* 363-384.

Butler, E. & Kaiser, E. (1971). Prediction Of Residential Movement And Spatial Allocation. *Urban Affairs Quarterly, 6, 4,* 477-494.

Butler, S. (1985). *Privatizing Federal Spending.* New York: Universe Books.

"Clinton Pushes Homeownership Strategy." (1995, June 6). *The Washington Post,* p. A-17.

Cox, K. (1982). Housing tenure and neighborhood activism. *Urban Affairs Quarterly, 18, 1,* 107-129.

DeParle, J. (1991, August, 29). How Jack Kemp Lost The War On Poverty. *New York Times Magazine*, pp. 11, 26-27.

Ditkovsky, O. & van Vliet, W. (1984). Housing Tenure And Community Participation. *Ekistics, 307*, 345-348.

Doling, J. & Stafford, B. (1989). *Home Ownership: The Diversity Of Experience.* Aldershot, England: Gower.

Dreier, P. & Atlas, J. (1992). How To Expand Homeownership For More Americans. *Challenge*, March-April, 42-47.

Farmer, M. & Barrell, R. (1981). Entrepreneurship And Government Policy: The Case Of The Housing Market. *Journal of Public Policy, 1*, 307-332.

Fischer, C., Jackson, R., Stueve, C., Gerson, K & Jones, L. (1977). *Networks And Places: Social Relations In The Urban Setting.* New York: Free Press.

Fischer, C. (1982). *To Dwell Among Friends: Personal Networks In Town And Country.* Chicago: University of Chicago Press.

Forrest, R. (1987). Spatial Mobility, Tenure Mobility, And Emerging Social Divisions In The UK Housing Market. *Environment and Planning A, 19*, 1611-1630.

Galster, G. (1983). Empirical Evidence On Cross-Tenure Differences And Community Satisfaction. *Journal of Social Issues, 28, 3*, 107-119.

Galster, G. (1987). *Homeownership And Neighborhood Reinvestment.* Durham, NC: Duke University Press.

Green, R. & White, M. (1994). *Measuring The Benefits Of Homeowning: Effects On Children.* Chicago: Center for the Study of the Economy and the State.

Guest, A. & Oropesa, R. (1986). Informal social ties and political activity in the metropolis. *Urban Affairs Quarterly, 21, 4*, 550-574.

Gyourko, J. & Linneman, P. (1993). Affordability Of The American Dream: An Examination Of The Last 30 Years. *Journal of Housing Research, 4, 1*, 39-72.

Hays, R. Allen (1995). *The Federal Government And Urban Housing.* Albany, NY: State University of New York Press.

Hughes, J. (1991). Clashing Demographics: Homeownership And Affordability Dilemmas. *Housing Policy Debate, 2*, 1217-1250.

Hunter, A. (1975). The Loss Of Community: An Empirical Test Through Replication. *American Sociological Review, 36, 2*, 537-552.

Jeffers, L. & Dobos, J. (1984). Communication And Neighborhood Mobilization. *Urban Affairs Quarterly, 20*, 97-112.

Johnson, A. & Sherraden, M. (1992). Asset-based social welfare policy: Homeownership for the poor. *Journal of Sociology and Social Welfare, 19, 3*, 65-83.

Kasarda, J. & Janowitz, M. (1974). Community Attachment In Mass Society. *American Sociological Review, 39*, 328-339.

Kemeny, J. (1981). *The Myth Of Home Ownership: Private Versus Public Choices In Housing Tenure.* London: Routledge & Kegan Paul.

Kemper, V. (Summer, 1994). Home Inequity. *Common Cause Magazine*, pp. 14-19, 26.

Linneman, P. & Megbolugbe, I. (1992). Housing Affordability: Myth Or Reality? *Urban Studies, 29*, 369-392.

Long, J. & Caudill, S. (1992). Racial Differences In Homeownership And Housing Wealth, 1970-1986. *Economic Inquiry, 30,* 1, 83-100.

Mayer, N. (1981). Rehabilitation Decisions In Rental Housing. *Journal of Urban Economics, 10,* 76-94.

McHugh, K. (1985). Reasons For Migrating Or Not. *Sociology and Sociological Research, 69, 4,* 585-589.

Merrett, S. (1982). *Owner Occupation In Britain.* London: Routledge & Kegan Paul.

Meyer, P., Yeager, J. & Burayidi, M. (1994). Institutional Myopia And Policy Distortions: The Promotion Of Homeownership For The Poor. *Journal of Economic Issues, 28, 2,* 567-576.

Oliver, M. & Shapiro, T. (1995). *Black Wealth/White Wealth.* New York: Routledge.

Page-Adams, D. & Vosler, N. (1997). Homeownership And Well Being Among Blue Collar Workers. (Working Paper No. 97-5) St. Louis, MO: Washington University in St. Louis, Center for Social Development.

Parcel, T. (1982). Wealth Accumulation Of Black And White Men: The Case Of Housing Equity. *Social Problems, 30, 2,* 199-211.

Perin, C. (1977). *Everything In Its Place.* Princeton: Princeton University Press.

Perkins, D., Florin, P., Rich, R. Wandersman, A. & Chavis, D. (1990). Participation And The Social And Physical Environment Of Residential Blocks: Crime And Community Context. *American Journal of Community Psychology, 18,* 83-115.

Pickvance, C. G. (1973). Life Cycle, Housing Tenure, And Residential Mobility: A Path Analytic Approach. *Urban Studies, 11,* 171-188.

Putnam, R. (1995). Bowling Alone: America's Declining Social Capital. *Journal of Democracy, 6,* 65-78.

Rohe, W. & Stegman, W. (1994a). The Effects Of Homeownership On The Self-Esteem, Perceived Control, And Life Satisfaction Of Low-Income People. *Journal of the American Planning Association, 60, 2,* 173-184.

Rohe, W. & Stegman, W. (1994b). The Impact Of Homeownership On The Social And Political Involvement Of Low-Income People. *Urban Affairs Quarterly, 30,* 28-50.

Rohe, W. & Stewart, L. (1996). Homeownership And Neighborhood Stability. *Housing Policy Debate, 7, 1,* 37-81.

Rossi, P. & Weber, E. (1996). The Social Benefits Of Homeownership: Empirical Evidence From National Surveys. *Housing Policy Debate, 7, 1,* 11-35.

Salsich, P. (1993). A Decent Home For Every American: Can The 1949 Goal Be Met? *North Carolina Law Review, 71,* 1619-1646.

Saunders, P. (1978). Beyond Housing Classes: The Sociological Significance Of Private Property Rights In Means Of Consumption. *International Journal Of Urban And Regional Research, 18, 2,* 202-227.

Saunders, P. (1990). *A Nation Of Homeowners.* London: Unwin Hyman.

Sherraden, M. (1991). *Assets And The Poor: A New American Welfare Policy.* Armonk, NY: Sharpe.

Silver, H., McDonald, J. & Ortiz, R. (1985). Selling Public Housing: The Methods And The Motivations. *Journal of Housing*, November/December, 213-228.

Stegman, M. (1993). *More Housing, More Fairly: Report Of The Twentieth Century Fund Task Force On Affordable Housing*. New York: Twentieth Century Fund Press.

Steinberger, P. (1981). Political Participation And Communality: A Cultural/Interpersonal Approach. *Rural Sociology, 46, 1*, 7-19.

Stone, M. (1993). *Shelter Poverty: New Ideas On Housing Affordability*. Philadelphia: Temple University Press.

US Department of Housing and Urban Development. (1992). *Home Ownership and Opportunity For People Everywhere*. Washington, DC: US Department of Housing and Urban Development.

US Department of Housing and Urban Development. (1995). Urban Policy Brief, 2, August. Washington, DC: United States Department of Housing and Urban Development.

US Department of Housing and Urban Development. (1996). US Housing Market Conditions. Washington, DC: United States Department of Housing and Urban Development.

US Department of Treasury. (1994). Statistical Abstract Of The United States. Washington, DC: US Government Printing Office.

Whitehead, C. (1979). Why Owner Occupation? *CES Review*, May, 33-42.

Yates, D. (1982). The English Housing Experience: An Overview. *Urban Law and Policy, 5, 3*, 203-233.

Index

Note: Page numbers followed by f indicate figures; page numbers followed by t indicate tables.

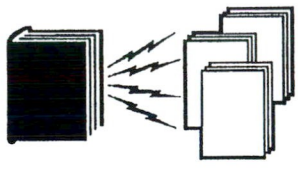

Haworth
DOCUMENT DELIVERY
SERVICE

This valuable service provides a single-article order form for any article from a Haworth journal.

- *Time Saving:* No running around from library to library to find a specific article.
- *Cost Effective:* All costs are kept down to a minimum.
- *Fast Delivery:* Choose from several options, including same-day FAX.
- *No Copyright Hassles:* You will be supplied by the original publisher.
- *Easy Payment:* Choose from several easy payment methods.

Open Accounts Welcome for . . .
- Library Interlibrary Loan Departments
- Library Network/Consortia Wishing to Provide Single-Article Services
- Indexing/Abstracting Services with Single Article Provision Services
- Document Provision Brokers and Freelance Information Service Providers

MAIL or *FAX* THIS ENTIRE ORDER FORM TO:

Haworth Document Delivery Service
The Haworth Press, Inc.
10 Alice Street
Binghamton, NY 13904-1580

or FAX: 1-800-895-0582
or CALL: 1-800-429-6784
9am-5pm EST

PLEASE SEND ME PHOTOCOPIES OF THE FOLLOWING SINGLE ARTICLES:

1) Journal Title: _____

    Vol/Issue/Year:_____ Starting & Ending Pages:_____

    Article Title:_____

_____

2) Journal Title: _____

    Vol/Issue/Year:_____ Starting & Ending Pages:_____

    Article Title:_____

_____

3) Journal Title: _____

    Vol/Issue/Year:_____ Starting & Ending Pages:_____

    Article Title:_____

_____

4) Journal Title: _____

    Vol/Issue/Year:_____ Starting & Ending Pages:_____

    Article Title:_____

_____

(See other side for Costs and Payment Information)

COSTS: Please figure your cost to order quality copies of an article.

1. Set-up charge per article: $8.00
   ($8.00 × number of separate articles) _____

2. Photocopying charge for each article:

   1-10 pages: $1.00 _____

   11-19 pages: $3.00 _____

   20-29 pages: $5.00 _____

   30+ pages: $2.00/10 pages _____

3. Flexicover (optional): $2.00/article _____

4. Postage & Handling: US: $1.00 for the first article/
   $.50 each additional article _____

   Federal Express: $25.00 _____

   Outside US: $2.00 for first article/
   $.50 each additional article _____

5. Same-day FAX service: $.50 per page _____

   GRAND TOTAL: _____

METHOD OF PAYMENT: (please check one)

❏ Check enclosed ❏ Please ship and bill. PO # _____
(sorry we can ship and bill to bookstores only! All others must pre-pay)

❏ Charge to my credit card: ❏ Visa; ❏ MasterCard; ❏ Discover;
❏ American Express;

Account Number:_____ Expiration date:_____

Signature: *X* _____

Name: _____ Institution: _____

Address: _____

_____

City: _____ State:_____ Zip:_____

Phone Number: _____ FAX Number: _____

MAIL or *FAX* THIS ENTIRE ORDER FORM TO:

Haworth Document Delivery Service	**or FAX:** 1-800-895-0582
The Haworth Press, Inc.	**or CALL:** 1-800-429-6784
10 Alice Street	(9am-5pm EST)
Binghamton, NY 13904-1580	